Ask the

Words of Wisdom & Comfort from Unexpected Sources

Incredible journeys told through
the eyes and souls of nature's wonders

Marilyn Geddes
Illustrations by Cynthia Mackenzie

Rattlesnake Books
Calgary, Alberta

Rattlesnake Books, Calgary, Alberta, Canada

First Canadian Softcover Edition
October 2007
12 11 10 09 08 07   1 2 3 4 5 6 7 8 9 10

Library and Archives Canada Cataloguing in Publication

Geddes, Marilyn S. 1948–
Ask the very beasts : words of wisdom and comfort from unexpected sources : incredible journeys told through the eyes and souls of nature's wonders / Marilyn S. Geddes; illustrations by Cynthia M. Mackenzie.

ISBN: 978–1–9783889–0–4 (softcover)

1. Spirit possession. 2. Shamanism. 3. Spiritual healing and spiritualism. I. Mackenzie, Cynthia M. II. Title.

BL2370.S5G43 2007   299.7'1144   C2007–905718–7

COVER IMAGE: *Surveyor of the Lands*, mixed media, 2007, Cynthia Mackenzie
EDITING: Sandy Gough, Calgary, Alberta
DESIGN AND PRODUCTION: Jeremy Drought, *Last Impression Publishing Service*, Calgary, Alberta
PRINTED IN CANADA: *Friesens Corporation*, Altona, Manitoba

www.rattlesnakebooks.com

Dedication

To Paul,
whose words helped build our foundation
and to Jaki,
friend and inspired teacher

Illustrations

Contents

CATS

WILD THINGS

OTHERS

Introductory Words

Ask the very beasts, and they will teach you;
ask the wild birds—they will tell you;
Crawling creatures will instruct you;
the fish in the sea will inform you;
For which of them all knows not
that this is the Eternal's way,
In whose control lies every living soul,
and the whole life of man.

from *The Book of Job*, Chapter 12,
as quoted by J. Allen Boone in *Letters to Strongheart*

The teachings offered in this little book have all come from Spirit, and as a result, are not from this ordinary world. Some years ago, I embarked on a shamanic path, and through the development of an innate skill that allows me to bridge the realms, I learned to communicate with the Spirit helpers I had come to know. Soon afterward, I discovered that the depth of connection I could achieve with this ability was one of my gifts. Being dedicated to a Path of Service, it was only a matter of time before I offered to help others in this way. The 'journeys' that I share here are the result of that work. My part has been to be open, to record clearly what is offered, and to stay out of the way with my own ideas, interpretations, and in particular my judgments of how the information will be received by those who have requested the journeys. Over time, I have learned to accept that these offerings provide a level of truth and support to others. It seems that even if the information is at first challenging, ultimately, it brings greater understanding and compassion, soothing the recipients and allowing them to be more generous to all aspects of Creation, and to themselves in particular.

Most important, the teachings clearly demonstrate, time and time again, that everything—*everything*— in our world has a consciousness and an ability to guide us, if only we ask. Some may wish to debate the truth or believability of the journeys. I feel no need to prove, argue, or justify, for it seems that what is offered is simply another perspective to commonly held views. It is not up to me or anyone else to label them *absolute* in any way. The key is to allow them as possibilities. If, when you read them, you are moved; if your understanding is enhanced; if your perceptions of the world around you shift; if you experience an expansion of heart to include more than you ever have before; if you are enlivened by stepping into Mystery; if you experience for even a moment the interweaving and interdependence of All That Is; your life will be enriched, as mine is with each journey. A reminder, though, from Paul, one of our dearest human teachers—"Remember, don't take it all too seriously!" Leave room for delight and laughter.

The illustrations have flowed through Cynthia as inspired and unique works of art. Allow the beauty and feel of each to weave through the words, deepening and enriching your experience.

Although most of the journeys have come from a variety of animal friends, domesticated and wild, we have included others that may surprise you. In addition, there are selected journeys drawn from the many I have taken during workshops and courses I have pursued, under the direction of my remarkable teacher and friend, Jaki Daniels. Superficially, it may seem the book lacks continuity, yet all is held together by its dedication to All My Relations, in whatever form, and with whatever words and visions they wish to present themselves to us, and through us, to you.

What is Journeying?

Author's Note

Used by generations of indigenous peoples, journeying is a method of accessing information from what is referred to as non-ordinary reality. When we state our intentions clearly, a journey can bring us information and guidance from what we might call a higher perspective. The messages are presented in words, images, and sensations.

When I embark on a journey, I first create a sacred space through ritual and quiet contemplation. With a drumbeat as my only companion, I enter the journey by envisioning myself in a small cabin in a woodland clearing. I imagine that I am sitting on a wooden chair that is draped in a buffalo hide. I state the intention to myself, then leave the cabin to 'travel' to one of the shamanic realms, the Lower World, where I meet my Power Animal, my main guide in the world of Spirit. Once I have shared the intention with him, he chooses the destination that will bring us to the being who will speak to the intention.

The information can be interpreted on many levels. It may take several readings, over time, to access the full depth of what is provided. Images, in particular, often act as metaphor, representing something far beyond the actual scenes described. A few journeys make reference to images or information given in journeys that are not part of this book. I have not removed them, for it is important to honour the Spirit teachers by including every word they offer. I ask for your indulgence, and apologize for any initial confusion that arises.

Marilyn Geddes
Calgary, Alberta
June 2007

Every living thing was seen as a partner in a universal enterprise. Each had an individual contribution to make to the general good, which it, and it alone, could supply. Everything lived for everything else, at all times and under all circumstances.

Humans, animals, snakes, birds, insects—all shared a common language. By means of this language all were able to express their thoughts and feelings freely on matters of mutual interest. From out of divinely bestowed wisdom, they could reason together for the common good, the common happiness, and the common fun.

J. Allen Boone, *Kinship With All Life*, p. 8.

Between Friends

Between Friends
(watercolour, 1994)

I have come to believe that time is not as it appears. Before I even met Marilyn I painted this, for quite a different reason. That project fell away and I stuffed the piece into a folder where it was soon forgotten.

Marilyn's Power Animal is the Diamondback Rattlesnake, and mine is the Red-tailed Hawk. Although this image depicts neither a rattlesnake nor a hawk, the physical and energetic similarities to each engendered a jaw-dropping episode when I dug it out of the basement files.

The two of us have such a great time working together on whatever comes our way. Our conversation is animated and lively. With the added gifts of insight and perspective that our Power Animals offer, the place from which we view the world stretches before us, all the richer and wider than when we stand alone.

Meeting My Power Animal

March 2, 2004

Many indigenous people look to animal spirits that act as protectors, helpers and teachers throughout their lives. Often, a particular animal presents itself as one's chief guide through the realms of non-ordinary reality. Typically, we refer to this as our Power Animal. When I formally began studying the Shaman's Path, I journeyed, with great anticipation, and a considerable degree of doubt, to meet my Power Animal. Here are the results of that journey.

INTENTION

Travel to the Lower World and ask to meet your Power Animal.

I TRAVEL QUICKLY TO THE LOWER WORLD, the pristine realm where many animal spirits can be found, and enter the aspen and spruce forest I have visited before. A pure, clear stream bubbles and gurgles off to the right. I stand, and as instructed, call my Power Animal. I see a red fox turn his quick and curious eye upon me, and I ask, "Are you my Power Animal?" He turns and disappears into the forest's undergrowth, and does not return. Next, I notice a doe browsing in a clearing on the opposite side of the stream, so I ask, "Are you my Power Animal?" She lowers her head and continues to eat, showing no interest in me at all.

I stand, wondering what my next step should be. Again, I call my Power Animal to me. Out of the corner of my left eye, I discern a lightning quick movement upon the ground, a flash of brown and black diamond scales, and am shocked to see a huge snake at my feet, head reared as if to strike. I am stunned, for although I hold no animosity towards snakes, I have no attraction to or experience of them, either. Immediately the word *Diamondback* comes. I remain motionless, but manage to ask, "Are you my Power Animal?" I sense 'Yes,' but ask him to verify by giving me a sign. Immediately, the snake, beginning at my feet, encircles my body, slithering upwards in a spiral motion. I clearly see the intricate scaled patterns and feel his weight upon me. I offer one last test—"Leave me, and return only if you are truly my Power Animal." The snake unwinds, and with unbelievable quickness, disappears behind a wall of trees. Instantly he reappears at my side, and again winds himself up my body. When his head is even with my face, he touches his closed mouth gently to my cheek, and I am overcome by such deep emotion that I begin to sob. There is no doubt; this is a joyous reunion of two beings lost to each other for some time. I anticipate with great gratitude that from this point forward, we will travel together.

Cynthia Meets Her Power Animal

I DID NOT FORMALLY JOURNEY TO MEET MY POWER ANIMAL. Some years ago, in a dream, he stood beak to nose with me. I remember his visit well, as his sudden and dramatic appearance startled me. I was reminded of an ancient Egyptian character that depicts a huge bird head perched atop a human body.

Once I connected with the shamanic path, my Power Animal reappeared. I wore his head as a hood over mine. His mantle draped across my shoulders, reminiscent of an animal skin from a Native American ceremony.

In the beginning, I felt that we observed the world separately through our respective eyes. In this way, I could tune into his unique perceptions and add them to my own. Now it seems that we see through the same eyes. His way pierces through the fluff—no downy undercoat here. I am like a helicopter hovering above a snarl of traffic. I see how the roads become congested as traffic moves inward to the city's core. At the same time, I can see the many roads leading to freedom. A clarity that cuts through confusion without judgment is my gift from the Red-tailed Hawk.

Working With My Power Animal

March 4, 2004

Once I had met my Power Animal, the Diamondback Rattlesnake, I was curious about how he would assist me. Sitting in the late winter sunshine on a stone bench in the woods at a friend's farm, I posed the question, and journeyed to receive the answer.

INTENTION

How will you assist me in our work together?

VERY QUICKLY, I TRAVEL TO THE LOWER WORLD and call my Power Animal to me. He comes, and offers the following clear, succinct answer:

"I can assist you with three things—transportation, challenge, and protection." He has proven, over time, to do so.

Because I have researched the characteristics and habits of both the Eastern and Western Diamondback Rattlesnakes, I am aware of their potential to be dangerous, and deadly. So I ask, "Would you ever harm me?"

"Only if necessary for your transformation," is the reply. I then ask if Diamondback is male or female, and I understand that it could be either.

Aware of reciprocity, I offer the snake a mouse. Even though he exists only in Spirit, he is happy to accept.

I ask Diamondback if he will ever call on other animals for assistance, and am told to expect Turtle, Firefly, and Snow Goose. Since that conversation, all three animals have shown up in the work we do together.

Finally, I inquire whether or not he might call eagles or hawks for assistance. The answer is "No, not now. These birds can eat baby snakes, so will not be invited into our work at this time."

I thank my Power Animal for responding so clearly to my questions, and we return to our respective homes.

Since the day we met, Diamondback and I have travelled and worked together. Every journey begins with his guidance, and he is there at the close of every adventure as well. He is an excellent navigator through the unseen realms, willingly offering his assistance in matters ranging from the mundane to the sublime.

To honour Diamondback, and to remind me of his constant availability, I wear an antique silver and turquoise handmade ring depicting two intertwined snakes. This ring came to me in the most magical of ways, and is one of my prized possessions.

How Do I Serve?

Winter 2004

Because the Shaman's Path is one of Service, towards the end of our three-month introductory course we each journeyed with the question below. What follows is the answer I received.

INTENTION
How do I serve?

I BEGIN THE JOURNEY BY APPROACHING THE CABIN. It is a dark, starry night. No longer racing and dancing, I am walking, slowly and calmly. I enter the cabin, note that the fire is burning in the stove, then sit and settle into the buffalo hide. Diamondback is here as well, a first occurrence. I stand and wrap a grey poncho around myself. Diamondback coils himself around me, and we leave.

We travel to the Middle World, into the woods, taking the forest path we have taken before. As I walk, I ask, "How do I serve?" Diamondback responds immediately: "Walk slowly. Feel each step. See—really look and see." I bend and look as if through a magnifying glass. I see the base of a poplar, with a neat hole pecked out, perhaps by a Pileated Woodpecker. I see an anthill. In this small space, there is much to observe. We walk on.

On my left, in a tree, sits an owl. I ask, "How do I serve?" The owl responds, "Access your own wisdom. Access your *own* wisdom. It is deep within. Walk on." The owl silently and magnificently flies away.

I walk on. A green tree snake hangs from a branch on my right. I ask the question, "How do I serve?" The snake replies, "Look deep, beyond the surface." He opens his mouth, wide, and I look in, past his fangs, and see a perfect faceted crystal shimmering deep within his darkness. "Walk on."

We walk on. On my left on the ground is a ladybug. I bend down and ask, "How do I serve?" She replies, "Recognize *all* your teachers. Walk on."

We do so. On my right is a deer. I ask the question, "How do I serve?" And the deer replies, "Cultivate gentleness. Walk on."

We are nearing a clearing. I see a native elder, a wise man, waiting there. Approaching, I ask, "Father, how do I serve?" He says, "You are already serving. Study the ancient ways."

He then gives me a blessing, and wraps a soft yellow deerskin around me. "Take this back to your cabin to have with your buffalo skin." I thank him for his gifts, and thank all the animals. I am at the end of that road.

The River

The River
(mixed media, 2006)

One day, I knew I could not paint another watercolour. The desire to do what is called Mixed Media had been gnawing incessantly. I had to give in despite my fear. I had no idea where or how to begin. I felt like I had to leave everything I knew and begin all over again.

My teachers arrived in the form of the elements—Earth, Air, Water and Fire. They taught me how to see differently and how to interpret that insight through symbolism versus realism. I learned to use unfamiliar materials and to include found objects. Many of my pieces honor the elements, as this piece does.

When I was studying to receive Kriya Yoga, a form of meditation, we would sing chants. One, in particular, spoke of how we were but droplets of rain; to the ocean we would one day return. In "The River" the water flows without beginning or end, spreading to engulf the whole of the painting and perhaps you, the viewer, as well.

Story of the North

Winter 2005

As part of our Medicine Wheel studies, each of us journeyed for a story to share on a cold winter's evening. This was given to me, and is now offered to you.

INTENTION

Please tell me a story that I can share to warm the hearts of my people.

MY POWER ANIMAL GUIDE, DIAMONDBACK, takes me to White Cloud, an elderly native man who is a wonderful teacher. I state the intention—to share a story to warm the hearts of my people. White Cloud asks me to sit in his clearing, on a log seat. The clearing is pristine. It is late spring; the translucent green of early spring is transforming into the bolder, deeper greens of early summer. White Cloud begins:

> It is good to ask for a story that will warm the hearts of your people, for at this time in your world, so many hearts are cold with loneliness, or frozen with fear, and even hatred. Some hearts know not the gentle touch, and so are hardened against all love and feeling. Look around this place, this magical temple where we are now gathered, and ask what it has to reveal to us.

Once these words were uttered, the clearing came alive. The presence of myriad spirits of many sizes, shapes, and feelings was palpable, although unseen. White Cloud's image receded, as one by one, others took form. And the words come…

This space where we sit was not always as it now appears. In fact, it was empty, lifeless, barren, and harsh in surface. One might imagine it was like this from time's beginning, and would remain so for eternity. But, as you see, this was not to be so. The unmanifested introduced form, and form began to dream. Form desired its own comfort, and even though this had no previous knowing or existence, the dream of comfort spawned this form's creation. First, it knew of Earth, and requested this barrenness be visited by the Mother and softened in a welcoming way. So contours arose, depressions, hillocks, and the downy grasses offering soft surfaces on which form could recline. Next it knew of shelter, so from the dream of knowing, rooted beings, trees and shrubs sprang forth. They anchored deeply for stability, and spread their canopies whose shadows softened the beating of the sun, and whose leafy overhangs diverted the harshness of the rains. In addition, they responded to the messages of the wind, be they soft or harsh, alerting form to what was being carried in its way. Next form dreamed hunger, and as well, a respite from its gnawing pangs. In gazing round, it noticed the smallest of plants with sawtooth leaves, under which clustered delectable and succulent red fruits. These offered themselves to form, yet some kept hidden to plant the seeds for next year's crop. And so it went. Each dream that form called forth enticed a new creation, which in turn became a manifestation of form itself. And so it has continued, and thus the beauty and self-sufficiency of this magical place endures. All exists, is supported, and is sustained by all else. Share this story with your people. Share this dream of desire, creation, sustenance, satisfaction, love, and the arising of new desires. The keys are in the balance and the gratitude. May it warm your hearts, and guide your visions.

And so end our teachings of the North.

Rolling Thunder, Rushing Water

Rolling Thunder, Rushing Water
(mixed media, 2006)

Pounding hooves and dust flying brought two old friends to mind.

My first ventures into the 'unseen' began in the company of a small circle of friends. Every week we gathered to explore strange new territories. We would begin each evening by calling upon two trusted guides to keep our little band safe and sound, no matter what trouble we managed to get ourselves into. To this day, when I think of them, I feel protected and comforted.

With much gratitude, I thank Rolling Thunder and Rushing Water.

Reggie's Journey

March 2004

Reggie's was my first attempt at journeying to a horse. When completed, the owner shared that the information provided was consistent with what she had received from an animal communicator some time earlier. This confirmation encouraged me to try other horse journeys.

INTENTION

Reggie is a Thoroughbred horse who, if approached head on by another horse when being ridden, will spin suddenly and uncontrollably, and take off running. What is the reason for this behaviour? What is the message of this behaviour?

I TRAVEL TO MY POWER ANIMAL and we embark on a Middle World journey to meet Reggie. We fly until we see Reggie in a paddock, at a facility west of the city. As we land, we meet a robin who indicates that he is Reggie's Power Animal. It is clear we are to address the intention to him, and he will provide the answer. He explains:

> In Reggie's lineage is a horse who battled in mounted combat. He was taken from a peaceful pastoral environment, suddenly and with no warning, and sent to war. Very soon, he was in front line assault. In terror, he witnessed and felt other horses falling injured and dead to each side of him, but there was no escape. The enemy bore down, and this horse was killed in battle.
>
> This *memory* has passed to Reggie, and lives in the right side of his brain behind his right eye. He has, then, no control over his reactions to the oncoming horse. It is important that you talk

> to him, telling him you understand. Let him know that with this understanding, you will make sure to avoid direct confrontation with other horses. When you are approached, you will bear to the left, turning him slightly left to release the tension of a head on encounter. Use relaxation techniques yourself; your tension, as you know, transmits instantly to Reggie.

I remember that Reggie had been on the racetrack in his younger years, so I ask if anything happened in his life at the track that would add to his discomfort. I was told there were no additional problems there, or with his previous owner.

At this point, we thank the robin for the information, and return from our journey.

Doxie's Journey

August 8, 2004

My good friend Leah is a remarkable horsewoman who puts the well-being of horses above all else. She uses an instrument called an Acuscope to treat a variety of equine ailments. Curious about the process of journeying to speak with horses, Leah wondered if Doxie, one of her patients, would have something to say.

INTENTION

Doxie is a sorrel mare with laminitis, a disease of the sensitive laminae of the foot. A friend who is treating her wishes to know what Doxie would like to say at this time.

I TRAVEL WITH MY POWER ANIMAL down a gravel road that leads up to a house. We turn left in front of the house and head to the paddocks and fields. Once at the paddocks, we are met by a Jack Russell terrier who says that he is Doxie's Power Animal. He gives us permission to speak directly to her, but says that first we have to have some fun. At that, he jumps on Doxie's back, with no reaction from her. He then dances and performs many tricks for us. When the performance is complete, we speak with Doxie. Here are her words:

> This condition did not begin here at this place. It happened first when I was about seven, and has worsened each year. I know you wish I could be useful, that is, that I could carry you. That is your way of seeing me as useful. (*She blows through her nostrils.*) I am not complaining. I have not minded carrying you, for as you have been told before, that is the agreement between

> horses and people. But there are other ways for me to live. I am happy here with my friends. I love the warmth of the sun upon my back. I love to stand with my feet buried deeply in soft, moist earth. I love this life. You cannot bear pain, and feel compassion for me. Pain is not acceptable to you. For me it is different. Pain is part of who I am now.
>
> I have other gifts. I am easy to love and can help people open their hearts. Bring those to me whose hearts are closed, who cannot speak from pain or anger or fear. Through me, their hearts will open, for they will speak to me.
>
> Practically, provide no oats to me, just fresh, fresh hay and clean water.

I see salt crystals mixed with something, maybe pellets. I ask about pellets, and am told—"I will eat them when I am hungry, but they are not so good for the body. I prefer good, clean hay."

At this point, I ask if there is any more to be said:

> Thank you for what you are doing—that is, all the treatments you perceive are easing my pain. Please do not try to fix me, to make me useful. I am useful, but in other ways.

Annie's Journey

June 2004

Laurie is another remarkable horsewoman friend. She and her horse Annie had been together for some years, but their relationship was not always smooth! Laurie thought a journey to Annie might offer valuable information. Laurie invited me to her property to work with her and Annie together. Together, we posed the following questions:

INTENTION

What teachings can you offer Laurie and I about working with you? Laurie states she has riding issues coming up. Can you comment in order to assist her with these?

I TRAVEL WITH MY POWER ANIMAL on the back of Snow Goose out to the ranch where Annie lives. She is lying down, but stands to speak to us. She gives permission for us to work directly with her; we do not need to work through her Power Animal. We are aware of her as a very clear, conscious presence with something to say.

> Our heritage is freedom but we have entered into partnership with you. When working with us, it is important to let go of all thoughts of domination. Tomorrow when you greet me, do so as an equal, not a superior. Pay attention to everything I do. Even the shaking of a fly off my head can be significant. Laurie wants something from this exchange, but she may not receive it. Something else will come instead. When you are with me, speak to me directly. Minimize your speaking to each other.

I ask what my own intention should be in working with Laurie like this. Annie replies,

> There is only one intention—to see the truth. I will show you many things, but your job is to see them. Again, this you may not be able to do.
>
> Pay attention. Feel things as I do. Did you know that I feel every nuance of the ground I walk on? I feel the messages of the wind. My skin is sensitive. Feel as I do.

Next, I ask Annie the question regarding Laurie's riding issues. Here is what Annie provides:

> Laurie's issues are related to conflict, insecurity, and anger. Laurie is so sincere. She wants deeply to be good and do good. There still is a conflict between her traditional self and what she knows inside. This has to do with paying attention outside of herself to the expectations of others and the desired outcomes of others. She believes this is necessary to make money in her business, for she fears business will go if people don't get what they want. This is not so. There is a way to work from within what she really *knows* to be right. This is necessary.
>
> The insecurity relates again to the conflict. Again, we recognize Laurie's high degree of sincerity in her work. There is too much dependency on the thoughts and opinions of others, being afraid to act with confidence. Laurie needs to connect most deeply with herself in stillness, to feel what's here (*I see a vision of Laurie touching her heart and solar plexus*), not what's here (*I see her touching her head*). It will not come from thought and trying to figure it out. Sitting a few minutes a day by water and gazing west to the horizon—empty—will be very helpful. Laurie thinks she is too busy to do this; the busy-ness will ease, but she can start this practice now, every day.

> The anger—some of it is old. Again, Laurie wants to be perfect at this work with horses; the anger is mostly towards herself. Do you see how it all is woven together, the conflict, insecurity, and anger?

I ask how I can help. Annie replies,

> Just be there. She trusts you and you can be trusted. When you feel your own self tighten with answers or advice, breathe through that. The answers will come with me. Be easy with everything.

At this point, Annie turns away, indicating the journey is over. I thank her on Laurie's behalf as well as my own, and we all return to our respective dwelling places.

> *Spring 2007—When I contacted Laurie to ask her permission to include Annie's journey, I received this short response:*
>
> *Oh my gosh! I finally re-read Annie's journey. How amazing is that? It is the exact journey I have been on the last three years. Wow!*

Bastiaan's Journey

December 7, 2004

I met Katrina at a Shapeshifting workshop with John Perkins at the Omega Institute in the summer of 2004. We discovered that we had similar loves—dogs, horses, log houses, and spending time in Nature, and we have stayed in touch since that time. At Katrina's request, I journeyed to her elderly horse companion, Bastiaan. so that she could better support him as he aged.

INTENTION

How is Bastiaan doing physically, mentally and spiritually? Is there anything Katrina can do for him? Is he enjoying the Reiki treatments that she gives to him? He has a cough, and Katrina would like to know if the cough is painful or distressful in any way.

I BEGIN THE JOURNEY WITH MY POWER ANIMAL who directs us through the woods in the Middle World. On our right, we see a pasture or large paddock. There are some horses in it, more than one it seems. In the pasture is Bastiaan. I recognize him from the picture, a big boy. We approach quietly on his left. He looks up curiously, not alarmed, and goes back to grazing. He lifts his head, and looks straight at us, as if he knows that we have come for some conversation. I look around and do not see his Power Animal; Bastiaan seems to want to speak directly. I state the above intention to him, and wait to see if he will speak to us.

Bastiaan comes over and nuzzles my hand, as if he's used to receiving a treat, a horse crunch, or something. He steps back, and I ask that he consider the questions posed. He speaks:

Katrina is a beautiful woman with a beautiful spirit, and I am uplifted whenever she visits with me. I sense that within her is a deeper worrying, a worry about my well-being, a fear that she may be pushing me, or asking me to do those things that are beyond my capacity, or that cause me distress. She is sensitive to me, sometimes over-sensitive, I feel. With regard to the question of how I am doing physically, I would say that overall, physically, I am well. As you know, there is, off and on, some lameness, which affects my strides, and is certainly an inconvenience to the free flow of my movement, yet I have lived with this for many years, and in some ways it has become a part of who I am. I cannot control its outward manifestation, the way it looks to others and what they may judge about how I am feeling when I am afflicted more or less with the lameness. And yes, if I am pushed too hard, if I am asked to do too much, if I am used for too many hours of the day, a deep weariness sets in on that side and I wish to be left to rest. The pain is a deep pain, and perhaps, in your words it would be better to call it a deep, deep ache, for it is not the sharp pain that one might experience from stepping on a nail or ripping one's flesh on a protruding bit of cladding or wire. I am not expecting, I have no expectation that there will be a change in this situation. As I have spoken, I am familiar with this for many years, and I am also, myself, moving into old age. I do not have the capacity to recover as a young one might, so readily. But if you watch me when I am turned free, you see that my movement is not impeded, you see that I can hold my own with others of my kind, you see that I am not picked on nor seen as one to be shunned because I am too old and too near death. The others of my kind are easily accepting of me, and in fact, some do look to me for guidance. It is often my response that is attuned to first, should something unrecognizable, unknown, or alarming approach or occur. The panicky responses of the young are no longer part of my makeup, and it is my presence that can quell those responses in others of my kind. So, no, the lameness is not a problem. It is as if my body has had a shift that I must bear.

Katrina asks how I am doing mentally, and again I say that mentally I am strong, my mind is strong. I am not fumbling, or stumbling, or feeble in this capacity. I have the intelligence to respond to those directions from the riders who sit upon my back. Even when those directions are confusing or unclear, my experience allows me to choose the action that most probably will bring them pleasure with my response. When Katrina rides me, I feel the intensity and seriousness of her purpose, her wish to get things right, her wish to communicate so clearly with me with her hands, her body, and with her legs. This she does, to give me every chance to be on balance, to anticipate correctly, and to move with as much ease as is possible for me. I would remind her it is important to keep her head up, for every tip of the head towards my neck does weigh more heavily upon me. When her eyes are forward, and her head is upright, and she is straight and balanced in the saddle, that is when we communicate most smoothly and most beautifully with each other. I still enjoy the work I do for your kind, and am not yet ready to be turned out to pasture completely.

Katrina wonders how I am doing spiritually, and in a way, this is your word and not my own. What I can offer her is this: I feel connected to the brotherhood and sisterhood of horses, even though we are removed from our original way of being, where our ancestors ran free, collectively, without the hindrances of servitude imposed by man. Although we are so removed from that, and are confined and regimented according to the needs of our human masters and owners, our spirits recollect and are connected to those times, and give us strength, and bring us a lightness, even in periods that may be heavy for us. Sometimes when I am standing, with my head lowered, seemingly asleep, perhaps I am asleep and dreaming, as you put it, I am recalling how it is to fly with my brethren, to fly and then to rest, to eat, and to drink of the cool waters, to live in perfect harmony and rhythm with all creation. I have, in past times, lived in just such a way.

Katrina has noticed that I do have a cough. The cough of a horse racks the entire body, is felt throughout, and carries such a painful sound to it. I have observed that humans at this time feel so helpless, there is nothing to administer or to do, but simply to let us pull up short, and give us time until the spasms have receded. I could not say that this is painful, but I must say that it is distressing and uncomfortable to be wracked by these tormenting spells. It seems they can be triggered both by dust and by exercise. And yet, so often, once we have continued our work, they ease, and I do feel better. I feel that it is important to mention that the quality of the feed affects the cough. Sometimes feed loses its freshness and is dry and dusty. This type of feed does not suit me well. Perhaps if Katrina has anything to say here to anyone who controls this, it is to remind them that the freshest feed of some good quality is best not only for me but for all those of my kind.

Katrina asks if I enjoy the energy treatments which she gives me and I would say yes; yes, I feel a deep appreciation for the times that she lays her hands upon me, in silence, and asks the energy to flow to those places in my being that are in need of both support and healing. The warmth of her hands and the energy they transmit move through me, and I can feel the resonance along my limbs and throughout my being. This is a wonderful gift that she gives to me, and I do hope, that in her closeness to me at these times, she is feeling the gift of appreciation and gratitude I am also giving to her.

I'm asking Bastiaan if there's anything else, if there's more information he'd like Katrina to have, and he's actually thanking her for a few things. He's saying that one of Katrina's strengths is that she has very good hands. Her hands are very gentle and easy on the bit. He wants her to know he appreciates her lightness of touch upon the reins, for it allows him to do what he can do best. He wants her to know this is really appreciated, and to keep her awareness of this. He also wants her to know that he senses that she worries quite a bit about him, and feels helpless around him, not understanding what he wishes, what would be best for him. The best thing she can do for him is to simply spend time with him, and to do it in a way that is joyful for her. Her joyfulness adds to his well-being. He asks that she continue to develop her sensitivity to him, that when she is working him, to be aware of the subtle signs that he is tiring, that he has had enough or even too much. He is willing to serve, as faithful horses are taught to do, and often want to do, and he will be available for more years to come, should he be treated with sensitivity and an awareness of when he needs to work, and when he needs to rest.

I'm asking if jumping is a possibility for him, and he's pretty well indicating that it is not something that he wishes to be doing at this time. He enjoys the work that is being done, but he also says that he enjoys any opportunity to see new places, to be out of the ring, on the trail, in a pasture, to just explore. These are the things that interest him.

I see him now with you, Katrina. You are standing by his head, and he knows that you care for him because he's dropping his head, in comfort and trust as he stands with you, completely relaxed. I ask him if there are any last words. He is saying he feels complete, and again, reminds you not to worry, not to take him too seriously. I thank him for his words, for spending time with a stranger. He turns and walks away.

Tom's Journey

April 6, 2007

Katrina's new horse is a bay Thoroughbred named Tom. After working with him for a few months, Katrina wondered if his health was completely sound. In order to investigate this, she requested a journey to Tom.

INTENTION

At this time, what teachings can you offer Katrina about your health and well-being? How can she best support you?

I TRAVEL WITH MY POWER ANIMAL, the Diamondback Rattlesnake, to a paddock where we see Tom. We know him from his photo. There seems to be at least one other horse nearby, maybe two or three. We approach Tom. I glance at my Power Animal, and note that he has transformed himself into an energetic form, as he has done with other horses. He explains that he does not want to frighten Tom with his rattlesnake appearance. Suddenly, a small, very noisy bird starts fluttering madly above Tom's neck. She is making a terrible ruckus, so we stop moving forward and I ask if she is Tom's Power Animal. "Yes, yes, yes," she chirps loudly. "What do you want from him? Why are you bothering him?" I explain that I am Katrina's friend who has come to ask about his health and well-being. She immediately fusses, "He's fine, he's fine. What do you want from him? He hasn't been here very long. He's still settling in. Don't you know that he's very sensitive? He's had some upsets in his life, and finally, everything's calming down."

I explain that we mean him no upset or harm. We've simply come to see if there are any messages he has for Katrina that will assist her in supporting him in every possible way. With these words, the bird finally settles down, perches on his back, and indicates that we can speak directly to Tom.

> It is true that I have a great sensitivity within my being towards everything in my environment, and within my physical system as well. How can it be otherwise? If you are at all familiar with my lineage, you will know that we have been bred by humans to provide a certain level of very intense performance at a very early age. This goes against our natural instincts and inclinations, where we abide at our mother's side for many months, that is until a new one comes to her. We are schooled not by humans with their intentions and plans, but by the mothers and fathers and sisters and brothers within our herd. We are then trained in the skills of survival that allow us to live in a wild and free way. So we are tuned to sun, to moon, to heat, to cold, to nuances of pressure and temperature. We feel keenly the vibrations of the Earth beneath our feet, and we turn our ears to any disturbance in sound that calls us to it. We have a capacity to scent and thus, combining this with all other sensitivities, we can be alert to our enemies in a heartbeat. We attune as well to those wiser ones in our herd, the survivors who are experts at reading the signs that instruct us of staying or moving, of danger or safety, of the absence or presence of food and water and shelter. So, when the signal is raised from any of these wise ones, we feel it instantly and react without question, for to linger in consideration might cost us dearly. Do you understand that although we have travelled long upon your planet, it is only in relatively recent times that we have been pulled from this natural way of existence? So, the sensitivities are still an essential part of our makeup.
>
> Now those of your kind have found ways to capitalize on our strengths, and on our sensitivities as well. We are built, it seems, to easily carry you; this we have been long trained to do, and do, for the most part willingly. It does bring pleasure to

us to provide service to you, for we are on the whole a gentle species, more comfortable with harmony than with discord. In addition, you have taken advantage of our natural instinct to fly at great speed. This we do on our own both for the delight of the movement, in particular when there are many who join us in this motion, and also to escape from any danger that may present itself to us. We have the capacity to cross even varied terrain with little faltering or falling behind. All works in harmony—our vision, our hearing, our breath, our scenting what the wind brings to us, and the urgent movements of our bodies as we stretch our necks and flow in fluid motion to we know not where until the urge is given that we must stop. In seeing us, what man would not be moved to harness what we have for his own pleasure and delight and enhancement?

And so those in my direct lineage have been born and bred for speed, agility, and yes, intelligence. What has suffered in the ever-constant push to develop us for your sport at younger and younger ages is an imbalance. First, there are the physical effects of stress upon bone and cartilage and sinew and muscle that being pushed too young too hard exacerbate. Then, there are the effects on mind and spirit. These sensitivities, then, that we have described as serving us so well in our natural state are, because of the manner of our upbringing and the early push to perfection, these sensitivities are for the most part quickly moved to high alert. Because we are confused and yes, sometimes harmed in your focused push for more and faster from us, we cannot rest. It is as if we are at all times at full vibration—we can feel it from within— even as we long for a meadow in the sun. Do you have some sense of this?

Perhaps we are exaggerating somewhat here, for there are many who raise us for sport who do love us and give us the very best of care. Remember though, they are viewing us always through the magnifying glass of what we might become. So even in their care, there is an expectation and a consequence that we do feel. We do, however, always appreciate the kinder touch upon us.

We recognize that we have spoken at length of something other than Katrina's question, but we feel an understanding of our words can only deepen her and your understanding of the state in which we find ourselves amongst your kind.

Katrina asks of my well-being and physical health. As my protector has so truly indicated, I am fine. I am fine. I am settling in here, and in Katrina I have found a kindred spirit. There is no doubt. I appreciate the willingness she shows to honour my being, while at the same time, moving me into new areas of skill and expertise and ultimately, pleasure of partnership. Again I speak of sensitivities. It is perhaps apparent that the drop into relaxation from that more accustomed state of high alert is somewhat inconsistent. There are times when I feel the rising within me of focused attention fully on Katrina and the task at hand. At other times, I am transported back to previous times within my life where the daily routines and pressures and jarring by so many with their varying demands set my anxiety at high alert. Katrina no doubt has noticed these times, and we appreciate that she responds with calmness rather than with upset or increased demands of her own. We thank her for this. And we ask for continued patience, for we are learning the new ways. Remember, though, that the areas that are deeply scarred may every once in a while be re-awakened. We can offer no guarantee.

With regard to my physical health—there are no great underlying problems that we can share with you. What we can describe is this: at times, I am taken more with a general sense of weakness. That is, rather than identifying a problem in particular limb or foot or shoulder or joint or internal organ, I do, at times, feel less than my full strength. I can only link this, again, to our sensitivities.

It's interesting here, Katrina. I keep getting a sense of Tom being really tuned in to the phases of the moon. He's not telling me this, but I see him standing in a stall at night. There's something about him that is responding to the night sky, in particular the full moon. It's not clear what to make of it.

The other thing he is showing me is that his overall constitution is somewhat weak at this time. There's nothing really wrong. It's just to acknowledge that this is part of his makeup. He'll do the best he can for you, but asks that you attend with your own sensitivity to those times when he seems to need more support. There is an indication that you might investigate some sort of supplement. It's weird, but I am seeing a white can or bucket of something, with a large green logo of some sort on it. Sorry, that's all I get.

At this point, I am asking him if there is anything else he'd like to say about his health and well-being. He does indicate that the source of his constitutional ups and downs are linked to his internal structure—his digestive system—more than any structural ailment. It's not that there is anything really wrong. He's just showing it, I believe, as an area of vulnerability.

I go over him with my mind to see if there is a call to any other area of his body, and he seems perfectly fine. I had wondered before I did the journey if he had any strain to his back or hips that might need a chiropractic adjustment, but he looks fine. He's had some wear and tear, to be sure, but he is good. There might be one little spot on his spine. Forgive my ignorance of horse anatomy, but it would be between the back end of your saddle seat, and about 4 inches further on towards the tail. You might just check that out. Otherwise, nothing.

I ask if there are any last words. He raises his head from where he's been grazing, and looks at us. "Thank you," are his final words. He drops his head again. The bird flies up, shooing us out of there. We thank Tom and his friend for the information, and we all return to our respective dwelling places.

Katrina replied the day after receiving the journey. Here are a few of her comments:

The journey actually makes great sense, and should be considered validation. Tom just recently was put on U-Gard, an ulcer medication that comes in a white tub with a green label. This has actually helped considerably with the symptoms that I had been concerned about a while ago. The general weakness I wonder about, but it makes total sense too. He was tested low-positive for Lyme disease which the vets do not generally treat. Around here it's something like 90% of horses have Lyme show up. This could explain why he feels so weak at times. Thought you would like to know.

Prince's Journey

May 8, 2005

Prince is a 26-year-old Quarter Horse who recently cut the pastern of his back right leg. His owner, Pat, is concerned about his well-being.

INTENTION

What does Prince need for healing? Are there any messages he wishes to give to his owner and companion of many years?

I TRAVEL WITH MY POWER ANIMAL and the other helpers south of the city, to a place where I can see Prince standing. He is resting his injured foot, putting weight on the left hind. He stands comfortably in the warmth of the day, head relaxed and drooped, dozing. He does not appear in any distress.

Arriving there, I see a small grey cat sitting on the rail of the fence. I ask, "Are you the Power Animal for Prince?" and she answers, "Yes." I explain our purpose, and ask if we might speak to Prince about his condition and his desires. The cat suggests we walk over and call to Prince, which we do. Prince responds to his name, looks towards us, and slowly ambles over. Again, he is slow, but does not appear to be in distress. I introduce my helpers and myself. He is not shy, but reaches his head towards us, and allows me to scratch his cheek, and then his neck. He stretches forward in obvious contentment at this attention.

I tell Prince that we are there at Pat's request, that she is very concerned about him because he has been looking so pained, uncomfortable and old when she visits him. Prince speaks to us.

> Please tell Pat that it has never been, and is not now, my intention to cause her any worry or distress. She has been with me throughout most of my life, and has shown me nothing but

loving adoration. From me, she has learned the ways of the horse, and has, for the most part, been an attentive and respectful student. Of course, as is the way with so many of you who love and work with horses, she has at times been impatient with my less than perfect responses to her requests, and has also, at times, not been completely clear in communicating to me what exactly she has expected. I am speaking of the precise and exact movements that you desire when we are working together in a refined athletic partnership. So, of course, we have had our moments.

Overall, however, I have received the best of care, and consistent appreciation and loving regard for who I am. This has never gone unnoticed or unappreciated by me.

It is important that Pat knows that this most recent injury occurred by what you would call an accident. There was no maliciousness intended by man or beast. What transpired was the result of the natural interaction of myself with those of my kind; in the tumult, I kicked out, caught my foot, and injured it. Yes, the pain was shocking, and it suited me to stand and make no motion. Had I, at that time, collapsed and moved along, making my transition, there would have been from me a complete acceptance. That is the way with our kind, and with those of us who inhabit the animal kingdom. But this was not to be, for caring hands did come to me.

Please recognize that I have lived a long and happy life. Contentment has been my most accustomed state. I have no quarrel with anyone. And, now that my pain has been addressed, I am content once again to feel the sun warm my back, to nuzzle with my close companions, to eat the sweetness that is offered to me, and to extend the comfort that I am able to do. This brings me great pleasure.

Pat asks what I need for my healing. Recognize that at this age, healing may not be so rapid as in one younger, so I ask that you, Pat, pay close attention to the healing of my wound. Provide the dressings and the care as they have been indicated. You know me well, and are aware of both the subtlety and clarity of our communion with each other. So, attend to that communication, and act if it is necessary. This is all.

You must know that your kind and gentle hands upon my skin, and your encouraging words will support me greatly. I sense your fear and sadness at the possibility of my suffering and passing, and I say to you, 'This is the way of all things'. We do not carry fear in our hearts in the way that so many of your kind do, nor do we anticipate our losses. So I ask that you relieve yourself of the anxieties that you are holding on my behalf; they are not necessary, and the weight of them bears heavy upon me. Rather, look through the physical, look through my sagging back and stiffening limbs, and cast your inner eye upon my spirit. It is forever young, forever proud, and always free. Remember this. Practically, it is better for me to have some movement, as standing still promotes a stiffening of the injured area, and other vulnerable parts as well. So, encourage me to move with you, and, in time, you may once again mount upon my back. Again, listen for my messages to you to gauge the progress I am making.

At this point, I ask if there are any other messages that Prince would like to give. Here is what he says:

Recognize that harmony amongst my caretakers has its own healing gifts. Work together, those of you who care for me. I will do my best to move into the fullest health that I can access at this time, if you work together to support me.

Please know that I am filled with gratitude for the life I have lived, and am yet living. I recognize you as one who has been sent to travel on this Earthly path with me, and I with you. We have been, and are still so very good together.

Indio's Journey

May 8, 2005

Indio, a 6-year-old Paint, is Pat's horse as well. He lives with Prince and is recovering from an injury sustained last August.

INTENTION

What does Indio need for healing? Does he have any messages for Pat? Has she been with him in previous incarnations?

WE TRAVEL ONCE AGAIN TO THE FACILITY where we met with Prince, and we see a fine-looking black and white paint, very handsome and extremely athletic looking. We recognize him as Indio by his blue eye. He does not appear as laid back as Prince, but has a more intense energy and a greater alertness. I look to see if we are to approach Indio through a Power Animal as well; none appears. It seems that Indio is quite able to speak up for himself. I would say that his nature is more assertive.

As we did with Prince, we approach the fence and call to Indio. He is not asleep, but awake, aware, and fully tuned to all the goings-on in his environment. He looks at us, but is not so quick to join us. It is as if he is sizing us up, wondering if we can be trusted, and also wondering if we might have something for him that would make it worthwhile to come closer. He is a very smart, savvy horse. He has the clear air of a confident leader who, although capable of being playful, will suffer no nonsense. In fact, although we have his attention, he does not yet come close enough for us to touch him.

I introduce my helper and myself. I explain that we have been informed of his injury by Pat, who would like to know how he is doing, and what, if anything, he needs for his healing. I explain also that Pat would like to be able to ride him once again, as it has been some time since she has been able to do so. We wait to see if Indio will speak with us. I make the request, and he speaks:

> I am not surprised that Pat has wished you to contact me, for I sense both her concern, and her eagerness to have me well and sound once again. I cannot blame her, for as you can see, I am young, strong, and willing to work in partnership with Pat to help us realize our potentials together. I am not ready, as my companion horse is, to lie in contentment in the sun. I have a strong desire, an impetus from within, to move, to run, to stretch, to sweat, to push to my limits, and beyond. This is my heart's desire. My spirit is not daunted by the unfortunate mishap that has kept me from wholeness.

I ask Indio whether he is in pain. He answers this way:

> My movement, as I feel it, is impeded. It does not flow with ease. There is a tenderness and irregular quality to my gait. (*He's showing me that he is limping.*) My body's memory recalls a time when this was not the case, but I am powerless to make a change. It is as if this new way of moving has become my natural way. More than pain, there is what you might call discomfort, a knowing that something is not right. Again, it may be permanent; this I do not know. I am aware, however, that more efforts might be made to investigate the reason for this condition. Rest has not achieved the desired result; perhaps it is time to look further afield, to consult other experts who may have fresh ways of assessing and assisting my situation. (*He is now speaking directly his owner, Pat.*) Would you consider this? Speak to those who know, who have investigated, who have experience, and who may be open to what is not conventional. I would greatly appreciate this, as it will enable me to fully enter into partnership with you once again. I long for that opportunity. You are good for me.

I speak on Pat's behalf and say that I am quite sure that she will do everything he desires to assist in his recovery. He replies that he cannot promise anything; the condition may be irreparable, but he is not willing to give up, and asks the same from his owner. I tell him I will pass this on.

I ask if there is anything else he needs for his healing. He says again to his owner,

> I sense your worry and concern both for me and my dear companion, and acknowledge that, with your kind, such feelings are not uncommon. Amongst our kind, though, they are quite foreign. Use your concern to impel you to act on our behalves. In doing so, your energy will be activated, and your spirits will lift. This will benefit us all. The heaviness of your worry and concern does not augment our moving forward. You are strong and capable; in this way you are like me. Let us blend our energies to learn what can be done in an active, energetic way. (*I receive an image of Pat doing this. She is out there, reading, calling, talking to people. She has let the sadness and concern go. She is a woman on a mission!*)

I thank Indio for his directness and clarity. I also tell him how beautiful I find him, and share with him that I am an owner of a paint horse as well. He seems to bask in this adoration, although he's still a little reticent and held back. I ask if there's anything more to say, and he says, "No, not at this time." He is eagerly waiting to see what happens next.

At this point, I look over to Prince, and ask him to join us. I then speak to both horses, saying, "Pat has previously been told that she has shared other lives with one or both of you. She is wondering if you have any knowledge of this, and if so, will you share what you know with her." At this point, I wait to see what happens.

Indio turns to Prince, gives him a quick nudge, and allows him to approach us once again. He does, however, stay close to Prince, in a position to push himself between Prince and us, if that should seem to be necessary. I wait to see how they consider the question.

It is Indio who speaks.

> Have we known Pat before? The answer is yes, although not in the way you might anticipate. With your kind, you are of the opinion that your individual spirit, or essence, is eternal and can, by will or invitation, inhabit a succession of physical forms. We do not hold the same understanding. For we belong to the collective of *Horse*, and it is to this that we return. Our individuality is melded with the whole of horse consciousness. We do not choose our incarnations. It is as if horse consciousness moves seamlessly through and beyond all of our being. So yes, Pat, we recognize some familiarity in you. Each of us can sense that we have known you before as one who has associated with the consciousness of horse. Clearly, you were once a native brave. Your life depended on your horses, and you moved as one with each of them. Your worth, both for yourself and in the eyes of others, was determined by the stature of the horses that you held. It is the inheritance of this lineage that has brought you once again to love the horse in this lifetime. This perhaps will explain to you the strength and vehemence of your attachment to us.

I ask if there is more that they would like to say on this subject. Although Indio has spoken, it is clear that Prince has been in complete agreement with what has been said. They do not seem to need to say more.

They have just given me another picture. You are living in an earlier time, in a city. It may be London, but could very well be New York or Boston. It is a time of the horse and carriage. You are dressed for a ball or some other fancy social event. Your coach and four horses are awaiting you. You have blond curls ornately piled on your head. You are wearing a pale pink gown, long, with full flounced skirt. The neckline is scooped. There is a kind of feathery, lighter pink ruffle around the neck. You are being helped into the coach, but have stopped to put your hand on one of the horses and say a quick word to him. You enter the coach, the door is closed, and you move off into the night.

At this point, Indio turns Prince away, and the two of them move off towards the back of the paddock, noses snuffling the ground. I take this as the indication that the conversation is completed. I thank them for the wealth of information, and acknowledge that all will be passed on to you. They look around for a moment, as if to say thank you.

The journey is complete. I thank my Power Animal for facilitating this meeting, and we each return to our respective dwelling places.

Spring 2007—I have recently heard from Pat. She reports:

Prince is now very old—29 years old to be exact. This last winter was hard on him, especially in April with the cold snaps; however, he is looking splendid now, much like the 3-year-old he was when I bought him. Indio is now sound after spending a year running free on a ranch! I am riding him—love him as much as ever and he is still a challenge. I now also own Rufus, a 6-year-old whom I bought when I thought that Indio would never be sound. So we are a happy little tribe.

Java the Great

Java the Great (mixed media, 2007)

I met Java on his first day in the world. Marilyn and Leah had been up all night with the vet, working to save his life and that of his mother, Patchy.

When I arrived that afternoon, they had left the darkness behind. There was Java, rushing to explore everything from the woodpile to the farm equipment. Leaping and rearing, he showed no regard for his tired mother who was struggling to stay close.

This painting hangs in Marilyn's retreat room, where the little one keeps his ever-curious eye on her. Java remains so very happy to be alive.

Patchy & Baby's Journey

June 20, 2006

When I was about two years old, I moved with my mom and dad to a new district that was situated on the edge of the prairie. Every so often, my father would treat me by taking me to a farm, a riding stable really, so I could be led around on a pony. Through junior high and high school, I hung out at riding academies, working in exchange for free rides, or, on occasion, a riding lesson. At age 16, I acquired my first horse, Sassafras. Since then, I have rarely been without one, or two, or three horses.

Patchy is my current horse, a smart, sturdy white and brown and black registered Paint. At the Shapeshifting workshop with John Perkins, Patchy entered into one of my journeys. Although I cannot recall the intention of the journey, I clearly saw that Patchy would give birth to a little stud colt with similar paint markings. Two years later, on June 24, 2006, this little guy was delivered, exactly as envisioned. His registered name is Café con Leche, but we call him Java.

Here is a pre-delivery journey taken, at the suggestion of my teacher and friend Jaki, to Patchy and the baby she carried for 11 months.

INTENTION

Please may I enter into the relationship that exists at this time between Patchy and her in utero baby so that I may receive any available teachings.

I TRAVEL TO MY POWER ANIMAL AND STATE THE ABOVE INTENTION, asking too if this is possible. He indicates that it is possible, but difficult. Then he laughs and says that he is just joking, that it is not difficult at all, but we will need Snow Goose today for transport. Instantly we are flying high above the Earth with Snow Goose. We circle above Patchy, who is turned out in the field, even though I know that in reality she is locked in her pen. We land, and Diamondback transforms himself into a soft warm glowing light, which I hold close. He explains that he does not wish to scare Patchy with his Rattlesnake appearance, so he has made himself more soothing and attractive. Patchy sees us, and walks up. She gently leans her head into me, and I feel the communion that we share. I state the intention to her, and am instantly aware of the foal within her, curled in on itself. I see a white blaze, and some white stockings, but of course, my mind comes in and suggests I am making this up. Who knows? Patchy begins to speak.

> This relationship is about the exquisiteness of love, it is about weight, about mystery. This being that I enfold within me is of me. My blood informs him. My blood circulates, bathes him and enlivens him. This blood, this liquid love, knows no boundaries, flowing in uninterrupted fashion from one through the other, from one to the other and back, in a never ending circulation. What is carried in my blood is more than nourishment. It is the necessary knowing that must inform this child of mine so that he is prepared, when he drops from the womb into the harshness of separate existence. This knowing came to me in the same way through the being that carried and birthed me, and in the same way, to her, from her mother as well. And so it goes, backwards and forwards in time, no beginning and no end, endless information." (*I am shown what looks like a ribbon of DNA. Etched upon the DNA are little scribblings, and I know these are the stories that must be inherited by each successive generation, the instincts and knowings that relate to Horse, and that give shape to the common identity of all horses.*)

I ask Patchy if there is more. I am given a sense of the weight of what she is carrying, the downward pull of the belly towards the earth, the splaying of the legs to accommodate the bulk, the softening of once firm muscles that allow the vulva to open and slacken, yet not completely. I feel two things—the weariness of the physical body, but at the same time, an incredible spark of aliveness and anticipation. And, there is a feeling of complete acceptance, almost a resignation to the processes of gestation and birth. All this is shown without words, demonstrated in sensations. There is no distress at all, but the body does crave comfort. She says that is why the massages feel so good. Although the urge is to lie down, this is not done. It is not yet time.

I ask about any final words, and I am given the message of "HUNGRY, all the time hungry." I see the nourishment taken in by Patchy instantly translated into growth of the baby. I can see it expanding before my eyes!

I am left with the sense of patience, of resignation, of weariness, but a complete lack of distress in any way.

I turn my attention to the baby, and ask if there are any teachings. There is a sense of paradox—the wisdom of the horse lineage that has been 'downloaded' to him through the 11-month gestation period, and a complete childlike innocence and anticipation. So it is the ancient and the new concurrent in this one being. There is also the feeling of safety, although this is not how it is experienced by the baby. For us, the word *safety* also implies its opposite—*danger*. For the baby, there is no opposite. This baby horse consciousness does not seem yet to have a need for words. He is simply floating in the wash of being, with no needs. Again, the word *needs* is not really correct; it also implies its opposite. The baby just is, in effect, in perfect bliss. Of course, I see him shift and move. It's getting really tight in there! Then he settles into being once more. It is not that he anticipates this will go on forever; he will be ready to respond, but only when all indications are provided that change is coming. He cannot even think of 'mother,' for that would mean separate, and he has no experience at all of separation. He simply is. There is nothing more to add.

At this point, Patchy turns and walks away to once again bury her face in the lush green grass. The baby closes his eyes and sleeps, lulled in this belly cradle, his home, for now.

I thank Diamondback for his assistance, and we return. Journey completed.

Daisy's Journey

June 2004

John had just taken over as manager of a large working cattle ranch in the rolling foothills of southern Alberta. His hired man Denny was new; he'd had problems at a previous ranch and was fired. But his skills with cattle were good, he wanted a fresh start, and John gave him one. Sadly, while under Denny's care, John's best cow horse, Daisy, mysteriously died. John was devastated. He wondered whether negligence on his own or Denny's part had contributed to Daisy's death, and he also wondered what deeper meaning Daisy's passing might hold.

INTENTION

At this time in John's life, what is the significance of Daisy's death?

I TRAVEL WITH DIAMONDBACK and a celestial herd of seven horses to the Land of the Dead. Eventually, we arrive in a mountainous region where a herd of horses graze. Daisy is identified, and we approach and speak our questions to her. She begins:

Yes, I have passed over and am with my herd now. I did not know beforehand that I held such significance for John. He looked after me and I served him. That is the way it is with horses and people.

John took me to a new place. It was not my home, and I was injured there. A poison grew within me. I lay down and could not rise. Now, I am here.

At this point, I ask for more, and am turned over to the celestial horses for additional information. They speak:

> Daisy's death was an accident, as happens with living things. There was no planned import there. But it is good that John reads this as a sign for he has been called to this land. Although he does not own it *on paper*, he has been given great responsibility. The land is sacred, and sacred is the work. The importance is planetary.
>
> It is true that the humans on this land have suffered strife, but the power of the land does rise above this.

There is the sense that the time of the humans here has been so small as to be almost insignificant.

The final words are offered:

> Each day, it is important to gaze at the sweep of the hills against the sky. Recognize that rather than a *doing to*, it is a *learning from*. The wind sweeps all clean.

I thank Daisy for her words, and she rejoins her herd. I thank Diamondback, and we part from each other.

Jake's Journey

2005

Cynthia's family dog was Jake, a large sweet tempered Akita who passed several years ago. Lately, Cynthia has been sensing Jake's presence, feeling him close by. She asks if Jake has any messages for her. This little journey provides the answer.

INTENTION

What messages does Jake have for Cynthia?

I TRAVEL WITH MY POWER ANIMAL and meet Jake in a woodland. I greet him, and ask if he has any words to pass along to Cynthia. Here is his response:

> I am here in my magnificence. I have never forgotten you. And I thank you for your love. I am always watching over you. Many a dark night, I have curled beside your soul.
>
> Move into your new work with grace, but remember to allow your fierceness. Remember, I was gentle, but I had a fierce heart.
>
> I watch over and remember the children.
>
> I am happy and complete in Spirit, but you need only whistle when you need me. Watch out for my kind.

At this point, another Jake-like dog appears, only smaller, a female perhaps. She stands beside him, but doesn't speak. I knew they travelled together, and that all was well. They turn, and walk away together. The journey is complete.

Surveyor of the Lands

Surveyor of the Lands
(mixed media, 2007)

Bailey was abandoned. He was about a year old when Marilyn and I arrived at the pound, hoping to find her a nice little female companion.

Having completely given up, Bailey sat, head down, shoulders drooped against the back of a wire cage. I called Marilyn over, saying, "Tune in to this dog. This is a beautiful dog."

So this very large, gangly fellow of unknown heritage went home with a very small woman, where he was to live a very large life.

Bailey has been Marilyn's closest companion, seldom leaving her side. He has journeyed with her in all worlds and has been her friend, teacher, protector and, on occasion, her nemesis.

With his welcoming and tender manner, he has helped open the hearts of many who have come looking for assistance. This painting shows Bailey on Marilyn's land in the foothills of Alberta. He is much older, but his senses are still keen, his mind is clear, and his temper sweet. His joy for life is completely contagious. He loves the land and he loves Marilyn.

Bailey will be standing guard for her, no matter what.

Kodiak's Journey

June 2004

Bill was a colleague of mine. He and his wife Bernadette were planning a vacation to Mexico, but were very concerned about the well-being of their two dogs. On a previous occasion, Kodiak had been left in the care of Bernadette's son, who had moved into their home to care for him in Bernadette and Bill's absence. The result was disastrous, as Kodiak had wreaked considerable damage on the house when left alone. Realizing they did not want a repeat performance, Bill was considering boarding Kodiak and his new 'sister' Basenji at a boarding kennel for a one-night trial period, before committing them to a longer stay. He asked me to journey to Kodiak to discuss this.

INTENTION

Bill has spoken to you about going to a kennel tomorrow night, then again for several nights later in the month. Please express your understanding of what he has said. Do you have any messages for Bill and Bernadette?

I TRAVEL WITH MY POWER ANIMAL, along with my own dog, Bailey, to Bill and Bernadette's home. We find Kodiak lying comfortably on the bed, his new sister dog beside him. A monarch butterfly appears and states she is Kodiak's Power Animal. I remark that I am surprised that an insect could *be* a power animal. She replies, "Technically, I belong to the order *Lepidoptera*. I am capable of transformation as you know, and this makes me quite powerful."

I state the above intention. Butterfly speaks:

> Kodiak understands what Bill has been saying to him. He is secure and confident enough in himself to withstand this change. He does love his home. He is treated so well that he plans to live here forever. He doesn't really have a picture of 'kennel' but he will be fine. He's glad his new sister dog will be joining him there.
>
> He may feel confused at first, but the excitement of the adventure will take over. It is exciting to go to a good kennel. He asks that whenever he is taken away from his home to the kennel, he be treated there with gentleness and respect. This is important. He'd like to have his regular food, too.
>
> He asks that Bill doesn't fake happiness when he drops them off. Say goodbye and leave. Don't linger. He'll be happy to see Bill when he comes home.

The butterfly continues, speaking directly to Bill.

> When you return and pick up the dogs, they may be tired or lethargic for a day or two, but do not worry. Excitement and change are tiring and may keep them from sleeping much at first. All will pass, and return to normal.
>
> The dogs are very grateful for all the concern you are putting into this.

With these last words, Butterfly flies away. As she does so, we call our thanks after her, and return to our respective dwelling places.

> *Bill reported that the initial stay at the kennel for one night went very well, as did many longer ones that followed. Early in 2007, Bill, his wife, and the dogs moved to Guatemala, where they are undoubtedly enjoying their retirement!*

Maxi's Journey

Spring 2004

INTENTION

Maxi is a dog who came from the animal shelter. She is a wonderful pet, but has a habit of crying whenever guests come, and also, when she is taken out of the home. What are the reasons for this behaviour? What can be done to address it?

I TRAVEL WITH MY POWER ANIMAL to Maxi, and am given permission to speak with her. She explains that she has had two previous homes. As a pup, she was somewhat neglected, more from ignorance and lack of direct supervision. Consequently, she was taunted a lot by children in the home.

From here, Maxi moved to the home of an older woman. She was loved, but for some reason, was not there long. Now she is with her current family. It is explained that the family is a family of secrets. All the family members feel safe at home, where they are close, and closed. Maxi feels this, and has taken on the responsibility to hold the safety at home for everyone. She sees this as her job.

When visitors arrive, they are, in Maxi's eyes, an intrusion into safety. There was also one instance that occurred when Maxi was taken out. Something gave her the sense that they shouldn't be away from home, and now there is a pattern of distress whenever she is away from the house.

It is clear that as the family heals into happiness, the dog will too. At this point, the dog is doing her job of carrying sadness, tension, and worry for the family.

Some guidelines are provided:

- When guests come, allow Maxi a safe place at the heart of the home, not as a punishment, but as a retreat.
- Minimize stress by leaving Maxi at home, unless it is absolutely necessary to take her along.
- Maxi loves the freedom of long walks, so make sure these are provided.
- Talk to Maxi. Tell her of your appreciation for the service she is providing to the family. When you are truly ready, communicate to Maxi that she no longer needs to do this job, that others will take the responsibility of caring for themselves.

At this point, we realize that the journey is complete. We thank Maxi, and return to our respective dwelling places.

Zeke's Journey

Spring 2004

Zeke's owner is a neighbour of Cynthia's. When Cynthia saw how distressed her neighbour was over Zeke's declining physical condition, she immediately suggested a journey.

INTENTION

Zeke's owner explains that Zeke has had severe abdominal/digestive problems since he was a pup. His energy is low; he alternates between neglecting his food, sometimes for days, and then bolting it down. Veterinary consultation and care have offered only temporary relief. What are the reasons for Zeke's problems? What can be done to help?

I TRAVEL WITH MY POWER ANIMAL through the Middle World to Zeke's home. A caged canary is in the room with Zeke, and indicates that she is his Power Animal. We ask permission to speak to her about Zeke's ailment, and she agrees. Here is what she reveals:

"Zeke doesn't think he matters."

We are shown what seems to be a past life scene. We see Zeke as a dog, but a yellow mixed breed mutt, pointy nosed, and skinny. He is living with a small nomadic tribe that moves their teepees across the prairies as they travel. Zeke is a tag along. He is not special to anyone. And, he is always hungry. He seems to belong to one man who is in his early 30s, but this man is rough and uncaring. The dog follows him, but when he comes too close, he is abused with words and kicks. On one nomadic move, the dog is injured in his left paw. He falls behind, and he starves to death.

At this point, I ask about the problems in this lifetime. I am shown a scene. Zeke is with a woman in the foreground, and I understand that she is his primary caretaker. There is, however, a man in the background. The teacher explains, "The dog feels too much attention, and not enough fun."

At this point, Turtle, who acts as my assistant, shows us a part of the intestine just past the stomach. There is an area of concern there, and it is indicated that the problem may be structural, or may be an ongoing irritation. The problem may be related to enzymes. I ask what to do, and see that Zeke is sent a healing by Firefly, another helper. Firefly cleans out the area, and fills it with light. From here, the light radiates until the whole dog is filled with light.

The words continue:

> Zeke is sorry that he is sick, sorry that he annoys his owners with his condition. He is in pain. He is not purposely upsetting them. He wants them to know that he knows they are trying. He asks that they focus more on his goodness than on his illness.
>
> Practically, wheat grass may be added as a supplement to his food.

There is a reminder that the way Zeke eats may be related to the past life scenario where there was never enough.

That was the extent of the journey. I thanked all the teachers who came forward, and we returned to our respective dwelling places.

> *After sharing the journey with the owner, whom I did not know, she offered the following information: Zeke had been diagnosed with an inflammation in his upper bowel, just below the stomach. The vet suspected enzyme imbalance. As well, just that day, Zeke had been invited to audition for a part in a movie. He would play a dog that travelled with a nomadic native community.*
>
> *2006—Zeke has recovered from all ailments, and is a healthy dog. His owner recalls that the above journey affected her profoundly, and changed the way she relates to her dog.*

Rusty's Journey

Winter 2005

We have known Mike since Junior High School. His kind heart bursts with love and pride for his aging small dogs. These dogs came to Mike when they were already elderly. They had been returned to the breeder years after they had been adopted, some because the owners were old and could no longer care for them, others because the owners simply could not bother with them any longer. Each time the breeder calls with a desperate request, Mike cannot refuse. So he always has three or four little dogs as his constant companions. Mike does everything possible to ensure they have the very best care. Recently, he requested journeys for two of them, Rusty, and Mickey.

INTENTION

Mike's 15-year-old Shitzu, Rusty, recently had an eye removed due to a tumour. His remaining eye is good. Mike is very concerned about Rusty's well-being. We ask: What are Rusty's thoughts and feelings at this time? Are there any messages that he has for Mike?

WE TRAVEL THROUGH THE LUSH, GREEN WOOD to where a little dog is lying on a small round dog bed on the forest floor. Above him, a mountain bluebird, brilliant in its colour, is watching over him, perched on a branch above. I ask the bird if he is the Power Animal for Rusty, and he indicates that he is. I look at the bluebird for any signs of weakness, but the bird seems healthy. We trust then, that this reflects the state of wellness of the one for whom he cares. The bluebird flies around us, dipping and diving playfully. When he alights on the branch again, I state the above intention. Bluebird begins to speak; it seems the answers will come through him. So we listen.

> As you can see, Rusty is resting. He is shown here in the woods, for the energy of the woodlands has a very healing effect on this little being. It is not that he needs to be taken to the woods, as such, by Mike, or anyone else. In our care of him, we are providing, through our beings, this woodland energy for it both soothes and invigorates. You can sense there are no threats here. There is only the power of the natural world, the trees, plants, insects, and animal life, the sun streaming through the leaves. All this has an influence on Rusty's spirit, his sense of his own well-being, and provides him the shelter in which to regain his strength.
>
> You can sense that autumn is in the air, and Rusty, at 15, is in the autumn of his life. This is not a time for tears, as autumn can be the richest and most poignant season of the year, and of a being's time upon your planet. So, Rusty's system is soaking up what autumn has to offer, and it resonates with the state of his own soul.
>
> The outward physical manifestations of Rusty's being are to be attended to, but not taken so seriously as to cause distress to Mike himself. Rusty is at home in his body, and for the moment, can adjust to the changes that the loss of the eye brings—changes in balance, perception, and ease in his movement. He has, as we might say, a blind side, and it would be good that all who care for him keep this in mind. Offer him no surprises from his blind side, but approach him from his sighted one. If this is not possible, alert him with a noise, or increase the weight of your footsteps so he can respond to the vibration of your coming.
>
> Any surgery to a being offers challenge and some distress to the physical system. In an older being, the recovery may be prolonged, and upsets to the system may take some time

> to regulate. Make sure to support the animal's system by providing those preparations that will aid his recovery. If his digestion seems upset, search for those preparations that will balance and enhance, in the most natural way, this system of the body. No extraordinary measures are to be taken. You might consult with a specialist in naturally restoring the physical well-being, a vet trained in this area. If you surmise all is well, then continue with the regimen that you yourself, Mike, have been implementing.

All this while, Rusty has been observing this exchange, cocking his head to use his good eye, and looking alert and very curious about the discussion. The sense that he is giving is that overall, he is quite comfortable, and happy not to be doing much. There is no feeling of suffering at this point.

I ask if there is any more to be said, and the bird indicates that all has been revealed. At this point, I ask if there are any messages from Rusty to Mike. At this, Rusty looks straight towards us, as if he is silently speaking. He says:

> Mike cares for me as if I were his child by blood, and of course, I am not. But I feel the degree of his deep love for me. I sense that in seeing me in pain, or in watching me decline as time goes by, Mike feels a terrible dread and a responsibility in tending to me to keep me well and alive. This deep love is felt by me, but I wish to speak to the pain I see in Mike himself.
>
> Mike, you owe me nothing. You have taken me in, cared for me, and loved me. You are not responsible for the natural processes of aging, and the individual challenges these bring to my system. The body is meant, ultimately, to fail, and no one can predict how that system's failure will occur. The body is meant, ultimately, to fall away, releasing the essence of the being, be it plant, animal, or human. We understand that it is difficult to watch the demise of one you hold so dear, but allow that the process is natural and ultimately needed. What we ask from you is to be supported with care and wisdom.

> We know that you dread the difficult decision of ceasing life if pain or discomfort appears to grow within me to the point where I cannot arise and take some joy from the day. I ask that, should you read these signs in me, you take the steps to end my suffering needlessly. It is a gift that you will give to me. I know that in your deep attachment to me, you will choose to take this decision only when the time is right, when you have sought wise counsel from others, and know that it is my time to shed the physical form. So please be easy on yourself about my care. All moves in a natural and fluid way around the never-ending circle.

I ask if there is any more to be said at this time. Rusty's only reply is a look, and a quiet expression, "Thank you." He then stands a bit shakily, moves in a circle, and settles himself more comfortably on his pillow. I turn to the bird and ask if there is any more. The bird flies low, circling over the dog, then returns to his branch. All is complete.

Mickey's Journey

Winter 2005

Mickey is also a Shitzu, almost 17 years old, and described by Mike as 'high maintenance'. His eyesight is fading, but he remains feisty, with a good quality of life.

INTENTION

Mike asks—Is Mickey uncomfortable or in any pain? Is there anything he needs from me that would add to his well-being? Does he have anything to say to me at this time?

I APPROACH MICKEY, who is lying on a pillow of folded cloth in a vehicle. There are two other dogs there as well. Mickey stands and turns around, then settles again. I see he is a little stiff, as one might expect in an older dog. He is alert and engaged when we speak with each other. I state the above intention, and also indicate that Mike has recently lost his dog Danny, which was very difficult for him. I tell Mickey that Mike probably has some concerns over his passing as well, that he worries how that process will be for him, as well as for himself. So I ask Mickey if he can speak to the questions we are asking.

Mickey tilts his head upward and cocks it slightly to my left. He looks very sharp and interested in this kind of communication. I start by asking him if he is in pain. This is what he says:

> I remember how it was when I was a young puppy. My body had boundless energy, I bounced through each day, so eager to see everything, taste everything, sniff all the wonderful smells of the earth, the grass, the people, and so many other animals.

> I never seemed to stop moving, except of course, when I would suddenly drop into a sound, sound sleep. Those days are no longer with me, but I remember how they felt, and in my heart, I am still that young one. You ask if I have pain, and I would say that it is not so much pain that I feel. What I feel is a loss of quickness, of flexibility, more stiffness, more slowness in getting up, sitting down, stretching, jumping. All those things I did without effort, all need now my focused attention. If I have any pain, it is in my left hip, but even this is so constant that it is almost a friend to me. Although I feel these things, I am not ready to stay still and give up movement in my life. You'll notice that I still have energy to call attention to myself by jumping up with my front feet on Mike's legs; he cannot ignore me when I do this!

I ask about his eyesight. Has he noticed any difficulties here? He says,

> Oh, am I losing my eyesight? I hadn't really noticed. Now that you mention it, there are clouds on the world when I examine it, but I have never depended too much on what I see. What I smell gives me so much more information. It is not my eyes that tell me where I am, who is near, what food is coming towards me. My nose is a finely tuned machine that constantly gives me information. I can also hear, and I especially like the sounds of humans speaking to me in soft and gentle tones. The rhythm of the voice—I can feel its effects throughout my whole body. So it is good to speak to me with caring.

I ask if there is anything Mickey might need from Mike that would add to his well-being. He says,

> Mike does everything within his power to keep me comfortable and well. I am aware that he scrutinizes me at great lengths, watching for any changes in my behaviour, my eating habits,

> even my eliminations. He takes me to see the caretakers who look after my health, and he follows closely any instructions they give to him about me. I could not ask for more. Sometimes, though, he offers me treats which are delicious, and which I cannot stop myself from eating. You know, we dogs must take what we can get as quickly as we can, without thought. This is related to our lineage, where we travelled and hunted in packs. The one who hesitated at a kill was the one who did not eat. So this urge is still strong within us. At times, I find the food that is offered may cause some discomfort in my system. I feel a pain in my belly and must curl up to feel better. So I ask Mike to be careful with what he offers me. He must be the judge, as I am the victim of my instincts. What I prefer is plain food.

He shows me a picture of chunks of meat and some vegetables. There is a bit of sauce or gravy on it, but I don't get the sense that it is heavily flavoured. He also shows some small morsels of what look to be fruit—peaches or mangoes, and bits of green grapes, of all things.

I ask him about dog kibble—he says some kinds are very good, and some are terrible, again indicating that they give him discomfort in his digestive system. He does show a bowl of it, though, so I'm guessing he considers it one source of good food.

I ask if there is more that Mike can do, or if he has anything to say at this time. He says,

> I wish to thank Mike for the love and care he gives to my companions and me, unendingly. He never tires of caring for us, when others have not wanted or have not been able to do so. We wish, though, that we could help Mike understand that when he is happy, we are happy. When he worries, we feel that as a weight upon us, and we try, in our way, to lift this weight. What we would like Mike to know is this—life is precious, life has its beauties and its challenges, life has brought us all together, and life is what animates each of us in each and every

> day. So the focus is, and must be, on life. Fear of the future, fear of the death of one of us, takes away from the life we are enjoying together, right now. We sense that Mike, and many others of the human kind, as well, fear death, because they cannot see into death and where it leads us all. I have within me a knowing that I will try to explain.

He shows me himself, running in a beautiful field. As he runs, he runs out of his body, and what runs on is lighter, but still distinct. This spirit dog keeps running, and joins up with many other such beings, all running and tumbling and falling and rolling together, so that it is almost impossible to tell one from another, where one begins and the other ends. But the sense is of complete doggy joyfulness. There is no distress, just an incredible sense of aliveness and lightness and fun. Then, different dog spirits leave the pack, run on, and again, are running in physical bodies, back in the field. I cannot explain what this means, as there are no words, but it suggests a knowing about death that we do not possess.

I ask Mickey if he has anything more to add about this, or anything else. Again, he says that he thanks Mike for the goodness he shows to him and the other dogs. He asks Mike not to worry or fret. They all have their physical challenges that come from age and genetics, they have their personalities and quirks and little nervous things, but all in all, they are very well. Finally, he says that although his teeth and gums are not what they used to be, he still likes those little coloured biscuits, and he would like to have something like them again! He looks up, cocks his head to the left, seems to smile even, and I know our talk is done. I thank him for being so helpful, and we return to our respective dwelling places.

Buck's Journey

Winter 2005

My dear friend Sherry called to request a journey for Buck, her aging and infirm wolf/dog cross.

INTENTION

Sherry has a sense, Buck, that you are in pain, that you may be longing, at this time, to make your transition from the physical plane to the ethereal plane, to join with the wolf and dog collective that is available to you. She asks if you wish to enjoy one more winter, or if you are ready to make your transition as early as tomorrow when you have a vet appointment. She would like your guidance in this matter.

I TRAVEL WITH MY POWER ANIMAL to the Middle World, where I see Buck resting outside his doghouse beyond the main house. There is a grey squirrel in the tree above, looking down on him, a squirrel that he might chase in other times. I ask the squirrel if he is Buck's Power Animal. He indicates that he may speak for Buck, and gives permission for Buck to speak to me directly. I state the journey's intention, and the answer comes from Buck:

> I come from a wild lineage, a lineage of the wolf, an important totem in a time when totems were regarded carefully for their significance. A wolf is a totem for the teacher, and I have come into the life of a teacher and her family, for an exchange of those lessons that are always available between animal and man, if both sides are open. My lineage is of the pack, the northern pack of which I was not able to be a part, due to the circumstances of my birth. I am aware that pack life is difficult

in this time of dwindling environments that are suitable to my kind, and yet the pack does offer such a feeling of belonging, such a feeling of one's place in the order of things. I came early to Sherry and her family, her son Nathan, and I have been a teacher to him in particular. It is through me that he became attuned to the natural ways, to the wild ways, to the ways that still stir his heart. It is through me that he has been brought to study my brothers as they live upon the land. It is the call of my kind that rings through his being, and asks him to be true to himself in a way that I could not be true to my lineage. There is no blame here. In many ways, it was fortunate circumstance that brought me to this family and this life. I have lived with those who have had some understanding of my nature, of that wild call within that could not be quelled, that could not be tamed, and I was given at times some outlet for it. Of course, sometimes I took that outlet without asking permission. I sense this may have caused some trouble.

The family became my pack, albeit a small pack, it was my pack nonetheless. And to this pack I did belong and do belong still. I have rested in the warmth and caring they have offered me, and I give thanks for them. I know that I am not what I once have been. I feel within me the flagging of energy, the longing to curl up upon myself in the cold snow and simply sleep. That is the way of my kind when we have that choice, or else to fall prey to an injury or an illness. Our passing may be wrought with pain and suffering, but this we understand is the way it is with wild beings.

You ask if I wish to stay on for another winter, and I say it makes no difference one way or the other. I understand your conflict and your pain when you must consider taking my life into your hands, but my life, in actuality, has always been in your hands. At any moment in our time together you might have decided that it was time for me to go. But that was not a choice you were drawn to make until now. So yes, my life is in your hands. That is our agreement. And yes, I am ready to go at any time. I feel no great longing to be here through the season of the cold. If you wish, I can stay for you. It is for you, please realize. For me it does not make a difference.

And so you wonder if you might assist me in this passage. I say to you that yes, you might. We have forged a strong bond, a bond of deep respect and deeper love. I cannot tell you what to do. The choice remains clearly yours, but I am willing to participate in whatever way that you decide. Should it be sooner rather than later, I ask that you be with me at the time of my passing. Although the natural way would be to be alone, as I have spoken earlier, we are not here discussing natural ways. And so, I invite you to be present at the moment of my transition. Recognize that what will be left behind is simply my wolf's clothing, that the spirit that animates this pelt will soon run free. I sense this may be very difficult for you, that your attachment in love and in respect to me will overwhelm you with the sadness of my leaving. This is the way it has to be. I cannot outlive you, but know that I am not too far gone to be able to touch you at some unsuspecting moments. Know without a doubt that I will do this. That is my parting gift to you. We have been good teachers for each other. Keep your heart open always to those of my kind. So much devastation is brought upon our heads by your kind, that every act of love and generosity benefits the whole. Keep your heart open.

I ask if there is any more to say upon this difficult subject and I am told, "There is great gratitude expressed for all of our being together. This I take with me, and this I leave with you."

I see the squirrel look down at Buck, and Buck curled on the ground with his head resting on his paws, coat looking ragged, but a great sense of serenity with him. He closes his eyes.

When she read the journey, Sherry acknowledged that she did not feel strong enough to be with Buck in his last moments. Instead, two days later, Buck was taken to the vet's by Sherry's husband who stepped in to assist this wonderful dog as he left his life on Earth.

Samantha's Journey

May 4, 2007

Joann called, distraught and in tears. Her 17-year-old Bichon companion, Samantha (Sam), had been failing for many weeks, and was obviously suffering. Yet Joann could not make the decision to assist Sam with her passing. She asked if Sam might advise her.

INTENTION

At this time, what teachings can you offer that will gently free both Joann and you from the tender ties of your long and loving relationship, thus allowing movement into your next steps?

I TRAVEL WITH MY POWER ANIMAL to the interior of a house where we see Samantha, a small white dog, lying on a blanket at one end of a sofa. Our first impression is one of shakiness. Samantha's life force is low; the cup is nearly drained. I kneel beside her, and very, very gently place my hand, barely touching, on the top of her head. My sense is that too much pressure will be distressing to her. Before I can fully state the above intention, she sighs and says, "Thank goodness you have come." At this, I state the intention, and we wait for Samantha to speak to us.

> It is true that for most of our years together, Joann and I have willingly been held by tender and loving ties. These have, as well, extended to her beautiful children. All has been very good between us. This last while, however, it is as if these ties have been replaced by an iron bond, so we are each held tightly, unable to move. Joann holds the key, but it seems she herself

has hidden it, and then conspired to forget its whereabouts. So we are locked in paralysis of suffering together.

We are aware that Joann is feeling heartbreak for two reasons. The first, and more obvious, is that from her human perspective, she is already grieving what she has known must come, and that is the absence of my warm and comforting physical presence in her life. For I have provided the solace, love, and acceptance to Joann that has eluded her when she seeks it amongst your kind. And of course, I have often entertained her! That is my job, that is the role of dog in the life of human, especially a dog such as myself with so many attributes that hold me as both being and plaything. I, and others of my kind, ask for nothing, yet accept with joy and gratitude whatever is offered to us. And we hold the one closest to us in highest regard for these offerings. Joann has been, in so many ways, an excellent provider, showering me with everything and more, to the delight and satisfaction of my doggy desires. I have accepted it all, with no disagreement whatsoever.

On a deeper level, there is another reason for Joann's heartbreak. True, the loss of the comfort I offer her is most obvious. What is not as obvious is that I have, through my open nature, provided the receptacle for her to give of herself unconditionally to me. Do you understand that I am the last one of her family to whom she could give and give and give, without expectation of anything but doggy faithfulness in return? Joann fears that when I have passed, she will close up into herself, in fear and yes, in some bitterness, and lose, except on rare occasions, that expansive and beautiful satisfaction she experiences when she opens her heart and gives to me. So she grieves my death, and she grieves as well the anticipated death of her own unfettered generosity. It is important that she understands this.

Yet what I am requesting here—and I must at this time speak clearly and directly to Joann—is release from the iron bond that holds us together. Neither of us is being served. Retrieve the key,

Joann, turn it in the lock, cast the bond away, and imagine that we are held by gently flowing pink and silken ribbons. Imagine then, that we begin to move away from each other. As we do, the ribbons stretch, then thin, and then begin to shred, ever so slightly. Eventually, they dissolve, and each of us continues our movement from the other, I into the realm where the Spirit Dogs await me, and you into the beauty of Life laid out before you. Each of us carries the remnants of the ribbons, but they are so light, weightless, in fact, that they cause us no distress at all. What remains is just the gentle brush of remembrance as the winds stir and lift them so they touch us. This is our reminder of the time we had together. It is as it should be.

Release as well the dread and guilt suffusing you when you imagine taking my life into your own hands by providing assistance for my passing. Choose one you trust in caring and in competence, and deliver me into their hands. For at this time I am easy with the relinquishing of the little life force that is left to me, yet eagerly anticipate the energy of release into the collective of which I spoke earlier. I am ready, and ask that you thank me, bless me, and let me go. In truth, I feel this as a liberation and a celebration. Let this be your last full and true offering to me. In return, I promise you that I will, that some aspect of me will, perhaps along with others of my kind, return to you and offer that light brush upon your cheek or leg or hand that will remind you that no matter what, you do not travel alone. Do you understand this?

It is time, Joann. It is time. Of course, nature, as you know, will eventually take its course, but the chances of increased suffering for us both are very high should no immediate steps be taken. I invite you to choose the way of freedom. Light a candle in our honour, and dedicate yourself to Life. In turn, I offer you my deep gratitude, and give you one small lick upon your nose. In this way, we are both very well.

At this, Samantha closes her eyes, and stays still. I realize she has completed her messages to us. I thank her for her honest and moving words, and wish her well on her journey. It's odd, but she seems to wink at me! I thank my Power Animal for facilitating this journey, and we all return to our respective dwelling places.

Once Joann had read the journey, she arranged to gather with her former husband and their two daughters to be with Sam when the vet came to their home to assist her passing.

Casino

Casino
(mixed media, 2007)

My dear friend, Laura, lost Casino, the last of her three beloved cat friends, a short time ago. I hope this small painting of Casino, sitting so peacefully in the warmth of the winter sun, will serve to remind her of how happily he lived, sharing her heart and her home, and of how close he remains—always.

Rex's Journey

May 22, 2004

Rex and Keldon are two cats who live with a man and his son. They are left alone a great deal, are confined to the basement rooms, but have access to the outdoors through an open window. Although they have litter boxes available, one (or both) of the cats is urinating in the basement, creating an offensive smell.

INTENTION

Why is this happening? How can the behaviour be changed?

I JOURNEY WITH DIAMONDBACK to the house where the cats live with the man and his son. Rex presented herself first, and we stated the intention directly to her. Her words:

> First of all, they've given me a man's name. This doesn't recognize my femininity. Second, I have had many lives. The best was as a royal cat in Egypt. At that time, I was a male. I fathered many children. I slept on a silken cushion, and I roamed free in the gardens of the palace of the Pharaoh. I was revered. When the Pharaoh died, I was killed—my throat was slit and I was entombed with him. This I did gladly.
>
> And now I am with this man and his son. There is an electric energy in the home.

I am shown a vibrating rope of electricity charging the air. It seems to come from the boy, but it is indicated that it is created by the father, passes to the son, and then to the cats.

Rex continues: "I do not feel honoured for being who I am. There is teasing and impatience. This electric energy is always vibrating here, and so I urinate." I mention that it isn't customary for females to spray, and she says, "I wouldn't know about that."

I inform her that the man has been talking of having her euthanized for this habit. She says,

> He should wash down the walls and floors. All scent must be gone. It takes so little for the invitation. Bigger litter boxes. Don't use that treated, scented litter. Plain clay, and mix some dirt in from the outdoors. I'll try that. Also, I need something to do—perhaps a scratching tower—a lookout so we can see out of the windows.

Finally, Rex states that she is the one who urinates outside of the boxes. Keldon is not guilty.

She then indicates that she has no more to say.

Keldon's Journey

May 23, 2004

I travel with Diamondback and Snow Goose to the Upper World, where we enter the Circle of Elders. We present our case to the Master, who is the leader of the Circle. We are sent to Frog, where we take time to connect with him. Frog speaks:

> Keldon is a softer, more amiable spirit. She feels the electric charge in the house, but is not so affected as Rex. Rex is generally aggravated and irritated by her status there in the house. Keldon is more easy going.
>
> Keldon loves the boy. (*I am shown a picture of the boy up front, with the father in the background.*) She loves the home she's been offered and feels comfortable and satisfied there. Rex takes the lead, and does most of the spraying. Keldon does little, if any. There may be a genetic 'brain' anomaly in Rex that allows this weakness.

At this point, Frog offers Keldon a healing for well-being and confidence. Frog blows on Keldon's head, three times, but his breath spreads to cover the cat's entire body. Then, Frog suggests I hold Keldon and envision myself as filled with light, passing this light through my hands to her. In doing so, we both become filled with light. I put her down, and she wanders to three of the other beings in the circle. She is stroked by one woman, licked by the dog, and then stroked by one of the men in the circle. She is relaxed and comfortable. Following this, we gather her up, and we leave on the back of Snow Goose.

Lucy's Journey

Autumn 2004

Nicole's male cat, unusually named Lucy, has passed on, with assistance. Nicole acknowledges that she neglected Lucy when she became very busy with her work. She feels badly, as Lucy was a cat who enjoyed attention and affection. She wonders if Lucy has any ill feelings towards her regarding this.

INTENTION

What messages concerning her life with the family does Lucy have for Nicole?

I TRAVEL WITH MY POWER ANIMAL, down, down to the gates of the Land of the Dead, and as promised, Diamondback arranges for us to enter. It is as I remember. We are wandering through the woods, a path in the woods, and we approach an armchair, the kind that would be in someone's living room. It might be brown or green, I can't quite tell, and on this is a cat, an orange cat, looking very comfortable and quite regal. I ask this cat, "Are you Lucy who lived with Nicole and her family?" The cat indicates that he is. I offer the above intention, and wait for Lucy's words.

I lived a very good life on Earth with the family. It was a family of humans and other four-legged creatures, some like myself and some larger. It was a house where certainly we knew we were central, we were important, sometimes the most important, and for this I am completely grateful. We had our warmth and our soft places, our food, and our opportunities to adventure and to hunt. This I liked very much, this adventuring, this hunting. I was led from my home by calls of interest and attention. I was led away by the feel of the bark as I scratched it, I was led away by the flutter of the birds that came to the trees, that came to the seeds, to the yard, to the garden. I was led away by the sounds of others of my kind yowling in the night, for I have a curious nature, and must see what is to be seen. I wandered freely, sometimes in the light and sometimes in the dark. Very little got in my way. I learned to crouch unseen, unmoving, except for the tip of my tail, while I watched in fascination those animals I might hunt. The watch was as important as the hunt itself. I felt very alive in those moments. And I could always return to that place of warm energy that was the hub where we all gathered. It was a hub where we belonged. I still hold the memory of the people who lived in the hub with me, the woman with her boys. It was a safe place, a good place, and yes, yes I am one who revelled in the warmth of someone's lap, a hand on my fur, stroking, stroking. And I hummed in appreciation of that touch.

I became adept at asking for that touch, and I could be quite noisy in my requests. For some time, the woman, Nicole, would gather me to her, and take the time to sit and stroke my coat in that pleasurable manner I have described. And so too her boys, and so too her boys. And yes, now that you mention it, those times together became less and less frequent, even though I continued to make my requests known. But you know we animals have a way of not holding on. I simply turned my attention to another, or to another pursuit. So no such thing that you might call resentment lingers here with me. Please pass this on. There is no worry, there is no holding of any animosity. And as you see, here I am, once again in comfort. I am free to rest, to roam the forest, to be on guard, to be alert, to never know hunger or fatigue. And I am one who is comfortable with this aloneness, and I can feel the presence of so many, many beings here as well. Many of my kind silently pass by. Occasionally we do acknowledge each other in a quiet way.

So yes, I am in a new place and a new time. I have not forgotten the old. All moved on, as it was meant to be. All moved on, all moved on. I hold images within me of my time on Earth with the family. And there is no discord within those images, only fond traces of pleasure. It was a good life. And I must remind you, this I know you know, but I must remind you once again, to remember that it is important to treat each animal being in your environment, to treat that animal well. And in doing so, you offer something to all animal beings in existence. There is much pain within the animal world. Many of my kind are dreadfully mistreated. And that is something you cannot help, you cannot save them all, you cannot be in all places of rescue at once. But we ask that in those you take into your home, in those you encounter in the street or in other people's homes, always respond with thoughtful kindness, with an honouring of the intelligence available to you if you would only ask. Recognize each animal has the capacity to be a teacher. Their wisdom is vast, you must only ask to tap it. So maintain your connection with the animals in your life. See us not as an inconvenience to be disposed of in difficult times. See us as beings who understand your communication far more than you could imagine. And of course, provide the physical care and feeding and safe environment that we need to walk in confidence in the world. It is not so very different for us as it is for you. We share the planet with you.

I ask if there are any last words, and am given a message of thanks for Nicole and her family for providing what was needed for Lucy's good life. And Lucy thanks her for recognizing his suffering, and assisting him to cross to this new world, even though it brought sadness to the family. He is available, and he says he visits now and again, so be alert for that. His final words are, "All is well." He puts his head down, and purrs. We thank him, and we leave.

I thank my Power Animal, and return home.

The Lion and the Lamb

The Lion and the Lamb
(watercolour, 1991)

Many are familiar with the teaching from the Bible that tells of a time when the Lion will lie down with the Lamb.

I had no idea the hold this image would have on me until its birth in a dream years ago. I had to put all else aside to capture the feeling of what I had seen. You may notice that the faces of both the Lion and Lamb have very human qualities.

To this day I treasure this little painting above all others.

Marco's Journey

February 2006

Marco is a successful entrepreneur and family man. Some years ago, he was informed, through dreams and fortuitous meetings with inspired teachers and situations, that he has deep links with a shamanic lineage that could be accessed in this time. Lately, Marco has a strong sense of his own mortality, and feels that he is, in a way, coasting, only scratching at his capacity in the greater Universe. He wonders what might be impeding his personal and spiritual growth, and asks that a journey be taken on his behalf.

INTENTION

At this point in my life, how can I fully utilize the gifts and capacities that I have been honoured with? What information, guidance, and support can you offer me that will illuminate my next steps?

The following is an excerpt from the clear and powerful teachings offered to Marco from the lineage of the Wolf.

I TRAVEL TO THE LOWER WORLD, where I meet Diamondback and state the above intention to him. We travel quickly, with the aid of Snow Goose, to the Upper World, where we meet my Spiritual Teacher by the stone bench. Again I state the intention, and he walks me forward to meet another teacher. Out of the mist comes a native man. He is tall and strong. What is most outstanding is that he is wearing the pelt of a Wolf, the head is draped over his own head, the pelt hangs down his back. He is dressed as if for ceremony. He wears a necklace of teeth strung on a leather thong. His hair is braided, and is mostly silver, although there are still strands of black. His face is wrinkled, especially at the corners of his eyes, like one who has squinted long into the sun, or smiled a great deal. His expression is solemn. Other than the pelt, he wears only a loincloth and a pair of laced moccasins that come to mid-calf. His chest and legs are bare. The air about this man resonates with contained strength and power, but there is no sense that he will misuse either. He approaches, and I ask if he will speak to Marco's question. He nods and speaks:

> Marco is correct in the information that he has received, that he is linked to a shamanic lineage. In fact, he is linked to an ancient lineage that reaches back for thousands of years in North America, and originally, on the Asian continent. The common thread throughout this lineage is the association with the Wolf, and the teachings that come through this magnificent animal. You see, I honour that connection by wearing the silver pelt of the male Wolf. In doing so, I honour this particular beast that came to me as a teacher, I honour the lineage, and I honour Marco in revealing its magnificence to him. In other times, in fact, he was familiar with this mantle of Wolf. He wore it proudly, and did not bring any disgrace to it. In a sense, we feel that if he were to take a moment to reflect, he will feel the Wolf's energy within, and surrounding, his own.
>
> What does it mean, in your time, to embody the intelligent knowing of the Wolf? One cannot, in your time, walk the streets of a modern city clad in nothing but a Wolf pelt, but in essence, one must hold that image in mind as one goes about his daily affairs. Let us look more closely at this lineage of the Wolf, passed through its people.
>
> First, the colour of this Wolf is a particular grey that is more akin to silver. The advantage is that, in the environments that Wolf has frequented, the colour can, of course, serve as camouflage, but there is greater meaning here. This particular colour has remarkable reflective qualities. One might gaze upon the Wolf but never even know it, for the ability of the fur to reflect the sun renders its actual form almost invisible to the

onlooker. This is clearly to the Wolf's advantage, whether it is travelling, feeding, mating, or leading the pack in the hunt. And this quality serves Marco as well. He can, like the Wolf, display himself as a strong and powerful player in the games of life; yet, he has the capacity, when he so chooses, to move as it were invisibly, even though in full view of those with whom he deals. In this way, he can manipulate outcomes to his own advantage, or to the advantage of those he represents, without enduring the scrutiny, criticism, or even bitterness that full disclosure might awaken. Can you see what a tremendous advantage this has been?

Another quality of the lineage is vision, a vision that depends not only on the eyes, but on the sense of smell, and on an inner sense of both direction and mission to be accomplished. If you imagine the movement of the Wolf, he does not wander, as does any one of the prey animals on which he feeds. He sets a course, is guided by the cues he takes from the environment that speak to this inner knowing, and moves with speed and with purpose towards the destination. If he fails, he rallies with the same purposeful determination that he set out with, and carries on again. His vision lives within him, always. And so it is with Marco.

We must mention too that there are those who clearly see the Wolf, and are awed and attracted by what stands before them. They are drawn to the magnificence of Wolf, and long to come closer. Even so, they know the possible consequence of doing so. For Wolf's embrace, although it may feel tender, is marked as well by tooth and claw. They learn, if they are wise, the balance between proximity and distance that will keep them safe. And Wolf acknowledges that he can be known, but never too well. Although this serves him, it also serves to keep him separate.

We could, it is true, further enumerate the qualities of Wolf that have some correspondence in the being that is Marco. However, we feel it would be more valuable to simply direct Marco to feel the resonance of which we have been speaking, to accept that the links are there, and to attune to them frequently. In doing so, clarity will come directly and quickly to him. We remind him, however, that the lineage has, as well, its vulnerable places. Wolf is a hunter, and as such, a hunter's well-being depends of course on his skill and experience, but also on the availability of those that serve as food. Because Wolf must always seek and seek for sustenance, there is little time for rest. In addition, Wolf is not a hoarder, as is the squirrel or the chickadee. So Wolf cannot rely on what he has saved, or put away. Always, always, once the hunger has returned, the hunt must resume, or life will soon be at an end. Although it goes against the nature of the Wolf, those within his lineage must seek for balance so they are not constantly exhausted by the ever present urge for movement and the seeking of food. Rest must be taken, goods must be put by so they can be accessed when conditions do not allow an easy access to the prey.

We see that for many years, Marco was as the Wolf, the hunter, thrilled and nourished by it, but eventually, recognizing that Wolf's ways would not always fully serve him. He has, in later years, learned from Wolf's vulnerabilities, and has prepared himself by stocking the larder to ensure security for himself and those he most closely cares for. Given this, Marco recognizes that the hunt continues, but the hunting ground has changed. Instead of looking outward to assist, to achieve, to conquer and accumulate, Marco is called to look inward to bring a richness and a fullness to his life. It is this that has been awakened by the recognition of his mortality.

Spring 2007—Marco wrote recently to say that he was preparing for an upcoming trip to Peru where he would be studying with indigenous shamans.

Weasel & Buffalo Journeys

Winter 2005

In the study and development of our personal Medicine Wheels, we each journeyed to meet our unique animal teachers. The first journey introduces Weasel, my teacher from the East. You will then meet Buffalo, my teacher from the North. Buffalo's words are amongst the most moving I have ever received.

INTENTION

Please may I meet my animal teacher from the East.

I JOURNEYED WITH THE DIAMONDBACK RATTLESNAKE, my Power Animal, to a campsite in the Middle World that I had visited before. I was instructed to lie down and wait for my animal of the East direction. This I did, but it seemed a long while before anything came. I felt a nuzzling of my hair, and when I turned, I saw a weasel. She acknowledged that she was the East animal teacher. I asked why she had come so hesitantly. She replied, "That is my way. I travel so very few notice, quickly, with little fanfare."

I asked for reassurance that she was the right animal, and she said,

> You have had your reassurance. Many people have never seen a weasel. You have eyes that recognize Weasel, because you have seen her many times on the land. That is how you know I am the one.

I then asked why, when so many others had winged teachers, I had a weasel teacher. Here is her reply:

> I am the animal teacher of the East because I approached you from the East. Although many people have winged teachers of the air, you are not one of them. This is the form I prefer.

At that, I watched the weasel spiral upward, changing into a hawk, an egret, a seagull, a swan, a heron, then back down to earth and again into a weasel.

Finally, I asked to perceive as Weasel does.

Here, I became Weasel, going back and forth from observing to being. The first perception came through the paws of the feet. They are so sensitive to every nuance of the terrain. Next, sight. As Weasel, I saw a mouse, and caught it in a lightening quick movement. I could feel the hot blood in the back of my throat. One or two bites, and it was swallowed down. Next, air scenting—tail high, nose in air, scenting moisture, and being led to water. Always checking the scent of the air—this was second nature. Then, feeling of touch upon the fur, through every environment. Stroked by grasses, thorns, branches, always aware of touch. Finally, suckling young—could feel the pressure of the milk and the tiny teeth upon the nipples. Exquisite relief.

INTENTION

Become the animal of the North. How does he perceive?

Buffalo speaks:

> My perception is more collective than singular. Although your eye may identify my outline as one distinct or apart, my perceptions are inextricably tied to the whole. By this I mean the herd of which I am a part. Those of old might have described the movement of our mighty herds across the landscape as a river, or an ocean, of beasts, so much were we one, and not a series of solitary beings. Even so today, though our numbers are low, and the herd may count as its members only a few, we operate as one body. What binds us is our wildness and our

Buffalo Man

Buffalo Man (mixed media, 2005)

I studied briefly with a Tibetan Bon Master who reminded me to listen to the rhythm of Mother Earth, which I think of as her heartbeat.

Every so often, a painting has so strong a life that, once engaged with it, I am transported from my everyday reality.

> The wind blows. Darkness dawns and I am flat against the ground. I listen for a feeling more than a sound. A deep low rumble surrounds me.
>
> I am cold. I smell his breath but I cannot see him. The rumble—the vibration of a multitude of his kind moving in the night—rocks the earth and I know he is close.

I do not plan to part with this painting. I lean on "Buffalo Man's" haunting presence to remind me of my real home.

connection to the land. Our hooves are supported, our mouths are fed by the grasses she provides us. The thirst of our black tongues is slaked by the waters she offers up. The winds to us carry mighty messages. They ruffle the hair upon our backs, and inform our nostrils of the subtleties of our surroundings and of any unnatural intrusions upon it. The wind notifies us of dangers, as do the tremors, however slight, of the Earth beneath our feet.

Have you ever observed my herd? Note how tightly we close together, always touching, sensing each others' heat and heartbeats. Despite your best attempts, it is fruitless and foolish to try to come between us and separate us one from the other. It is a dangerous game. Note how we turn with such quickness as one. You cannot discern leader from follower—the messages are received instantaneously.

Note as well the forbearance we carry. We have endured. We are not without the deep sadness that surrounds our losses. Recall that we remember how this happened and we hold you accountable. When you work with us, we demand your respect. We do not simply invite it. True, you still hold the knife, but know we do not submit. Our knowledge is deep, our wisdom is ancient.

Magpie Journey

January 12, 2007

In Alberta, where we live, many people express hatred for magpies, blaming them for everything from early morning sleep interruptions to driving away and even killing other birds, in particular songbirds. I've known those who routinely shoot and even poison these striking birds.

In our family, we like magpies. My brother David once told me that whenever he heard the expression 'putting salt on a bird's tail,' he would envision quietly sneaking up to the long black tail of a magpie, salt shaker in hand. When I walk in the woods, I feel welcomed and cheered by Magpie's greeting. I thought that investigating the true nature of Magpie might open people's hearts to the qualities of one of the prairie's most enduring indigenous birds.

INTENTION

What is the true nature of Magpie?

I TRAVEL TO THE LOWER WORLD, where I meet up with Diamondback, my Power Animal. We sit by the stream, and I explain why I have come. As we speak, we are aware of a group of magpies in the trees above, calling loudly to each other. One settles on a low branch to the right of us. He is almost too heavy for the branch, and it bobs under his weight and movement. He regards us closely by tipping his head and turning a keen, piercing, inquisitive eye on us. Unable to contain himself, he speaks:

> We are an ancient bird. Our true nature is survival. We are, of course, opportunist, taking what presents itself easily. As I have said, our true nature is survival. In this, how are we different

Holy Cow is That a Beetle?

Holy Cow is That a Beetle? (mixed media, 2006)

Oh dear Magpie, how we love you. Marilyn and I have long been loyal defenders of these marvelous bird people. No one really hears us though; hence, a proper introduction is in order. After you read the journey, we urge you to befriend the Mr. and Mrs. Magpies in your neighbourhood. They love to chat, and their particular logic has much to teach us.

from so many of you? Yet you judge us harshly and punish us with death at your hand.

We are noisy parents to our obstreperous young. Have you not noticed our clamour and attention and busy-ness once our eggs are hatched, and in particular, when our young begin to fly? We attend, feed, encourage, and stay in family for a long time, far longer, in fact, than many others of bird-kind. Have you not observed this? Do you not realize that when a flock of us, in speaking with each other, attracts your attention, we are a family flock? No one is ignored. Each one who calls receives an answer. It is only noise that seems chaotic. In truth, there is harmony in our association.

At this, I am shown a picture of other, smaller birds scrapping aggressively over food—physically wrestling with each other.

This is not the way of Magpie. Yes, there is a hierarchy that to the observant eye is obvious, but concession, when called upon, assists survival. We are focused, and, if you are willing, you can learn from our example.

With these words, there is a strong sense of family unit, a strong sense that they look out for one another, and a strong sense of intelligence.

We hold no animosity towards humans, but willingly co-exist and benefit from the association. We suggest that you humans take it all too seriously.

There is now a general sense of detached goodwill towards us, and an indication that if we focused on survival by taking what we needed when it was, through lack of others' vigilance, available to us, we would prosper and be easier within ourselves—more like Magpie! The last impression given is that Magpie is closely linked with Coyote's nature.

Coyote Journey

April 20, 2007

Because coyotes seem to find ways to adapt to the rapid encroachment of human populations into their territories, I wanted to speak to them. When I asked the teachers for an appropriate intention for our conversation, the following was provided.

INTENTION

What can you teach us of harmony?

I TRAVEL TO MY POWER ANIMAL and state the above intention to him. We fly through the Middle World, passing over habitats close to the city where coyotes dwell. We do not stop, but continue to the land south west of Claresholm where just two weeks ago, while riding, we spotted two large, healthy looking coyotes who were closing in on one of the small dogs who had accompanied us. They were bold, and even as we rode toward them, calling back the dog and shouting to frighten them away, they seemed diffident and unconcerned by our presence and our frantic actions. Eventually, the dog came back to us, and the coyotes turned and disappeared behind a hill. It is to these two coyotes that Diamondback directs me. We meet with them in the same general region where we had encountered them earlier, and I state the intention to them. As we wait for their words, I get the sense that both are males, and that they are, in fact, brothers.

You ask of harmony, as if that is something about which you need instruction. Harmony to us is synonymous with our natural state of being. We have, our lineage has, in fact, lived in this general region of the lands for many, many generations.

We have survived well, although not all times have been easy. We are kin with Magpie in our commitment to survival, and our ability to do so where others have not. We are perfectly designed to survive in a range of landscapes and climates; those offered here suit us admirably. Regard the colour of the hills. Does it not, in its subtlety of hue and rough texture, remind you of our coats that blend so easily with it? When we lie down to rest in these grasses, it is as if the land itself offers us a cloak of invisibility. You may pass close to us, but will never even know that we are there until startled, we jump up to startle you in turn. Yes, we can be taken by surprise, but not too often. Similarly, when we choose to stalk our prey, this camouflage of ours allows us to draw close and closer. This is to our advantage, although never a guarantee. We may lose the object of our hunt, and must turn our attention elsewhere.

Another aspect, then, of harmony, is patience. When one is lost to us, we do not lament, though hunger may be gnawing at our bellies. Instead, with our keen eyes, we scan again, hold still and silent, then strike when we are able. Of course, in spring and summer, we delight at the abundance of those small creatures who supply us with our lives. In winter, the waiting game goes on much longer. Again, we do not lament misfortune, nor dream of better times to come. We watch, we wait, we travel to what we hope to be more fertile territory. And, as all survivors do who depend on the hunt, or on the deaths of others, sometimes we die.

There are those who in regarding us might judge us far from harmony. The observer may note that when we travel through the lands of those we hunt, panic drives them to run and hide from us. How then, one asks, can this be seen as harmony when the hunter invades and then destroys the peace of those he seeks? We recognize that for those who hold 'harmony' as a benign concept of peace flowing without interruption, there is no choice but to see us as forces of disturbance and destruction. Yet, what is not seen is this: when our bellies are full and we are not in the mode to hunt, our passing is noted with alertness only. (*They reveal a vision, though, that suggests that they can, even when not in hunting mode, revert to it in an instant, if the mood should strike them. This brings to mind the 'trickster' aspect of their nature.*) It is only when our sight is set on feeding that it is felt by those we seek. Their activity increases, the call is sounded of our coming, and those that can, scatter and take cover or take flight. All are driven by survival. In this, there is a harmony.

Within your question is the deeper one of the enmity that has developed between man and those of us that you call coyotes. From our perspective, the enmity exists in one way only, from you to us. We hold you as no more or less significant as any other being we encounter. We have no interest in tracking and attacking you, for our preference and our suitability is to smaller prey. As well, you have found ways to arm yourselves with poisons and with guns that cause us painful injury and death. So, once we have experienced close contact with so many of your kind, we know it's best to stay away. Our preference is retreat into the wilder lands where your footprint is experienced less often.

We recognize however that the enmity begins when we seek after those that you yourselves have brought into our lands and raised to value, those infant and those helpless creatures in particular that you have introduced into our landscapes. Can you not see that through your blind trust, carelessness, or lack of vigilance, you have, in fact, offered something our opportunist selves cannot resist? It is as if you have acted in our best interests by providing such easy pickings for us! Have you no understanding of this? The assumption you arrive at is to blame us for taking the easier path when it is offered up before us, something you yourselves are most adept at doing. Yet, because you have set yourselves in opposition to anything that takes its own initiative to help itself, such as we do when we hunt those vulnerable beings you provide, you must declare us as the enemy, and seek our destruction as expeditiously, and often, as cruelly as possible. Such responses do not arouse our anger to retaliate. Simply, we increase our own wariness and vigilance, and learn to move amongst you in less visible and less obvious ways. As such, we seek to re-establish harmony with you, as you have, in fact, become a part of our landscape.

You will, we hope, acknowledge that our resonant partnership with the lands has existed through the times that did not include you in them. We have endured. And, even though you have, in some areas, brought concerted forces forward to ensure our destruction, we have found ways to thrive. Our lust for life is strong, our reluctance to relinquish our place upon the planet is resolute indeed. We have no need or desire to bring harm to you. We ask the same from you, but we do not expect it.

And now may we speak of our particular place here on this land that has so recently been inhabited by you, your kind, and your possessions? Know that we mean you no threat or disrespect. We have roamed here for many generations, have tolerated well the modest human practice of placing other animals within our midst and territory, and have hunted freely and openly, raising our young to full growth, and teaching them the complexities involved in sustaining themselves here. Our curiosity and our desire to maintain our patterns have brought us close to you and your habitation, but we do now understand that you will be amongst us for some time. We see the excitement you feel in our presence, we sense an underlay of fear, followed closely by the threat to us if we should meddle where you deem we should not go. We wish no harm to you, but remember our natures. Take care. Look after those amongst you that might be vulnerable to our quick and natural instincts to take what we can to survive. This is our reminder and our

> gift to you, the caution to take care. In doing so, you will honour the harmony that is the preferred state of existence amongst the natural beings. You will, in fact, join with us in attuning your awareness to the regions that are yours, those that are ours, and those that we must share between us. Allow that the boundaries are not fixed, they ebb and flow depending on so many circumstances—the season, the weather, the availability of food and shelter, our numbers, and yours as well. If we hold each other in some regard and respect, the two-way flow of harmony can be established and maintained. In this way, we bring little disturbance to each other. Allow as well that you can speak to us of your desires and preferences, simply by respectfully attuning to us with your deepest knowing. Wherever possible, we will comply.

At this point, it seems the teachings through words are complete. But we remain seated together, the two brothers, the Diamondback Rattlesnake, and me. We are easy and relaxed, we gaze west to the hills, and there is deep love and appreciation flowing amongst us all. The wind picks up, it ruffles the coats of the coyotes, and plays with my hair. I feel tears in my eyes, and I express my heartfelt thanks to these magnificent beings. Reluctantly, I stand with Diamondback wrapped round me, and say good-bye. The coyotes glance towards us, then resume their gaze to the west. We return to our respective dwelling places.

Autumn

Autumn
(mixed media, 2007)

In our part of the world, one frosty night can end summer. To celebrate the brief window of autumn, I love painting aspen in their golden halos.

Making mixed media pieces requires that I become a scavenger of 'things.' I seldom take a walk without returning with a fistful of branches or a pocketful of rocks. In the fall I must be a diligent collector. If I need particular lengths of twigs with certain diameters, I must stockpile before the snow comes.

Some of last year's treasures adorn this painting of my favourite beings—trees.

Wood Lily Journey

Winter 2004

The following journey supports the indication that everything in our world has the capacity to teach us, if only we will take the time to ask. This short journey was my first to a plant. Since then, I have visited others, and eagerly await each coming Spring to make the acquaintance of those that bloom as part of the original shortgrass prairie property that we have recently acquired.

INTENTION

Find, in your inner vision, a flower that speaks to you.
Ask: "What do you have to teach me?"

THE FLOWER I FEEL A KINSHIP WITH IS THE WOOD LILY, or wild tiger lily. I journey to the place on the land where we used to live, to the magical spot where I often found these beautiful orange flowers. I approach one, and this is what it says it has to teach:

Love. I love the Earth. My roots enter the Earth and branch into finer and finer filaments and the soil does no damage. It feeds me. I grow here because of the perfection of this place—the right amount of moisture, the richness of this never cultivated edge of the woods, the cool of the shade. But I have no knowledge that the Earth loves me. It doesn't matter. When I die each year and my colour changes lighter and lighter, I do give back to the Earth.

You feel badly because you don't come to see me in this place anymore, but don't. You can come anytime in your journey. You saw many of my cousins on the ridge last summer.

Your life is like mine. Your soil is formed from all the relationships that you've had—the substance of them crumbles together into this rich medium that supports you. Love this soil, as I love mine. It doesn't need to love you back. Like me, you grow in beauty, die back, and grow again. In this way, we are alike.

Summer 2007—I recently returned from a forest retreat where I worked for three days with Wood Lily to learn her medicines. When I posed the question, "What is your medicine?" I received the following answer: "My medicine causes one to swoon into the beauty of his or her own existence. It is difficult to resist my power." I was then advised, "Joyously work with me."

Under Wood Lily's guidance, I have prepared an essence to be offered, when indicated, to others. This is just one of several ways that I can joyously work with her!

Tree Journey

May 8, 2007

When I embarked on this tree journey, I had no idea where it would take me. I was pleased when we instantly travelled to one of my very favourite tree beings. We met 40 years ago.

INTENTION

From your place of endurance and wisdom, what teachings can you offer us today?

I TRAVEL WITH MY POWER ANIMAL through the Middle World to the foothills property where we lived for many years. An aging pine tree stands alone in a cultivated field, spreading its branches wide. Curiously, in shape, it reminds me of an oak, for it is so unlike the occasional pines that live alongside the towering spruce in the nearby forest. How did it get here? Was the seed carried by a bird, or on the fur of an animal, so many years ago? Was it deliberately planted? If so, by whom? These questions arise in my mind, just as they did when I first saw this tree many years ago, yet I am comfortable not knowing any more now than I did then. Diamondback and I stand in awe and gaze at the tree, then move slowly around it, appreciating it from every angle. There is a strong sense that it acknowledges us, for it is as if we can feel it breathing. For a few moments, it glows with a diffuse violet light; as it does, I feel warmth and tingling in my heart as I re-connect with this tree being I have loved for so long. I state the intention, and we wait to see if it will speak directly to us.

The teaching I wish to offer you today is of the visible made manifest through the invisible. I speak literally here, for the visible—my trunk and canopy—exists in harmony and interdependence with what is invisible to your eyes—and that is the sustaining network of roots that push relentlessly but respectfully through the Earth in an ever-expanding network that, through further and further refinement of its branches and filaments, is able to access even minute quantities of those nutrients so essential for my well-being. So many who gaze at what is visible, with wonder and appreciation, are unable to offer the same regard for this magnificent underground system that provides access to what is needed to sustain me—water, nutrients, and just as important, a supportive base. In fact, many observers of your kind in particular consider what is visible to be 'the tree,' and what is invisible, when they think of it at all, to be 'the roots,' thus bestowing upon us the dualistic nature that seems to define and guide the majority of you. Can you see what a misrepresentation of perception this is? For what defines us as 'tree' is the indivisible totality of being that includes roots, bark, branches, needles, cones, and all structural mechanisms that comprise these aspects, allowing each to fully fulfill its function in contribution to and participation in the whole. No one thing can be separated out and changed without an alteration to the being that is Tree. Please remind others of this when they consider that doing damage to any of our aspects will affect that aspect only. It would be just as foolish to suggest that lopping off one of your living limbs will leave the rest of the body unaffected. Through respecting each of us completely, you honour our magnificence.

Now let us take our words of oneness further. With your hand, gently sift through the soil that surrounds our roots. Note that very little grows within the shade we provide, yet there is life there still. Note the variety of insects that thrive at our base, and just below the surface as well. Such life, were you to dig deeply, would be apparent throughout the soil, living amidst our unseen underground network as well. Gaze at the bark of our trunk. What do you see? Again, life, and signs of life that have been here and then moved on. Note the birds that pause to nest or simply rest amongst our branches. They come, and then they go. Whatever the state of visitor to our system, we embrace it in the oneness that is us. In other words, we accept all, include all, and know that with these comings and goings, our essential being-ness adjusts accordingly. In this way we are, in each moment, born anew. Even you, when you approach us with appreciation and an open heart, are included in our system, for however long you choose to stay. And, we assure you that you need not be sitting at our side to join us in this way.

When you last saw me, you expressed amazement that I withstood the buffeting of the past winter's wild and violent winds. How was it possible that I, unprotected by other forest companions, survived when so many of them lay broken and toppled one upon the other? Much is owed to the expansive support of the invisible root system, much to the strength of my trunk that has been so fortunate to remain strong from within, unlike so many of my brothers' and my sisters.' Much is owed as well to my placement on this land. It was not accidental; deliberate hands did lay the seed here. (*I am given a vision of a child, a small girl, carefully planting the seed cone.*) Although the winds fly forcefully across the mountains and sweep down the hills towards me, the gusts that can destroy have for so many years respected my place here. As they rip through my branches, I give over to their strength, consider them yet another visitor, and allow them to become a part of me. Standing strong, I bow to their forces, rather than resist them. In this way, they know they have been welcomed. Then, they move on. And I then can delight that for that time, there was no separation between the winds and me.

We hope our words have offered you comfort, understanding, and some reassurance today. You sense that there is

> so much more we have to teach you, yet we will withdraw now to allow once again your reverence and your connection in us and us in you. Feel always the joyousness of our interaction.

At this, I know the journey is over, but I have been offered a hint of the many different teachings available from this magnificent tree being. I believe I understand, as well, how this tree has survived in a cultivated field, the only obstacle to the tractors and related implements that work the land from spring to fall each year. What do you think?

I thank this beautiful pine for spending time with us, and I promise to return. I thank Diamondback for accompanying me on this journey, and we each return to our respective homes.

Surprise

Surprise
(mixed media, 2006)

A chance encounter with a coyote late in the evening, a fearless young magpie's fascination with my toe nail, a butterfly landing on my finger tip, a magnificent bull moose silently crossing my path but a few steps away—these are moments that have changed me.

Several years ago, while driving back from a hike on a heavily forested road, three whitetail deer leapt in front of my car. Before I could catch my breath, they were gone into the darkness, the flashes of their brilliant white turned up tails contrasted against the deep gray of dusk. What a thrill!

Rock Journey

Winter 2004

It may seem almost impossible to imagine that rocks can be our teachers, until you experience what they have to offer. Because they are so dense, it is possible that we could journey to the same rock every day of our lives, and receive new teachings each time.

INTENTION

Choose a rock that calls to you. Connect to it first through direct contact by placing it upon your head or in your lap, then through a journey. Be open to any images and messages you receive.

I PLACE MY CHOSEN ROCK ON MY HEAD. Immediately, I see, or sense, a black channel move down through me to the centre of the Earth. Then, I am inside a vortex that starts above the Earth's surface and bores through to the molten centre of the Earth.

I am taken down through the vortex. I can see as we pass through the surface greenery, then through black soil, clay, sand, and rock with crystal bits in it. As I move further down, I enter the narrower part of the vortex, and cannot see much detail. The tip of the vortex enters the centre of the Earth.

Next, I place the rock in front of me, and journey to it. Immediately, the rock speaks:

Look how many of us there are.
Look how much we have to offer.
Look at how powerful we are.

Next, I am told that the vortex relates to me, that it is about working with people and animals. The words:

> Surfaces may look similar. The first layers are easiest to see. You may help remove or dig through these. All beings connect with vortices to the molten Source. We all come from the one Source. There is no wrong. Some of the vortices hit hardness and must bend, or split around it. But their connection is still there. Assist others to go deeper only by going deeper. You cannot do their delving for them. They will find a way to reconnect with Source. Once they connect with Source, they can fly.

Taylor House Journey

August 8, 2006

Our friends Ron and Anne live in an astonishingly beautiful two-storey house that is almost entirely made of glass. It sits amongst old growth Douglas Firs high on a Vancouver Island peninsula, looking to Georgia Strait and the mainland in one direction, and to Comox Bay in the other. Frequent visits from Island deer, quail, and pheasants reinforce their feeling that they, not the animals, are the ones being observed. The land itself holds a powerful and commanding energy. Since the moment that they took possession of the property, it has been the primary focus of their lives. Lately, they are feeling overwhelmed by the demands of upkeep of both house and land, and are wondering how to maintain their balance in this place.

INTENTION

At this time, what needs is this glass house fulfilling in each of us? How can we include its presence in our lives in ways that honour all?

I TRAVEL TO THE LOWER WORLD where I meet up with my Power Animal, the Diamondback Rattlesnake. I state the above intention to him, and wait to see where and to whom we will travel to receive the teachings. He indicates that we must sit down by the side of the stream. It seems he will speak to the questions, but I, ever the doubter, ask him again. He indicates he will provide the answer, for the question is *of Earth*. So, I wait for him to begin. He speaks:

> We use the term of *Earth* in referencing the above intention, for Ron and Anne's connection to the Land, and the structure built upon it, is in essence, of Earth. By this we mean that in

> establishing themselves there, (and they had no choice, we might remind them), in establishing themselves there, they were, in effect, deepening their respective connections to their Mother, the Earth. They believe so much of it is about a house, the glass house, as they like to refer to it, and their relationship to this magnificent man-made, yet inspired structure. And yet, it is the land that drew them to this very spot upon the planet at that exact time in their lives that they made its acquaintance.

At this point, I am shown a picture. First, it is the land without the house. Then, I see the house 'growing' in its place there. Next, I see a scene of some decay to the structure, then, Ron and Anne, your intense work to infuse it with new life and beauty. Finally, they show a scene of the house crumbling back to Earth.

> We are providing this vision early in our words to you so that there is absolutely no mistake. All WILL return to Earth, for dissolution is one step in Evolution. You believe that the pace at which this happens is up to you, and so you have exerted tremendous pressure on yourselves, and yes, upon the house as well. This pressure is from the Mind's belief that were it not for you, dissolution would proceed with lightning speed, and it is only your constant vigilance and efforts that will forestall this process. In effect, the house, which in itself holds a consciousness, feels this worry and this pressure, and is only too happy to fulfill your expectations. Please let us suggest to you that it can be otherwise.
>
> All is connected, organically and in consciousness as well. We know that each of you, in your own way, holds this knowledge, but we feel a dichotomy you have set up in your relationship to this magnificent place that you call home. You have infused your discussions of your next steps, steps you have chosen to make in unison, with so many *what ifs* about this place, and your place on it, that you have become quite crazed

> with confusion indeed. We ask that you adjust your language slightly here, for you are not so much on it, as *of* it. In other words, you have woven yourselves quite skillfully and deeply into this complexity and harmony of Earth, Sky, Water, Fire and its many systems—mineral, plant, animal, and spirit. And, you have done so with a focus and deliberation that is uncommon among your kind. And yet, we might say, you have, through the intensity of your discussions, your wanting to *create* balance and flow in your lives, lost sight of what you know to be true. Flow cannot be created. Flow is always there, always available. Imagine if you will, a beautiful meandering stream, constantly fed by a never-ending underground source that bubbles up from below.

They are showing me a scene of this. You two, as tiny beings, are floating on your backs in it, laughing and enjoying yourselves tremendously. Next, they show the two of you standing beside this stream, marvelling in the beauty of it, and the abundance that owes its life, in part, to the generosity of this never ceasing flow. You sit beside the stream, and you begin earnestly speaking. As you do so, one alternating with the other, picks up a rock and places it in the stream. Eventually you have created a dam, and the water begins to back up, forming a pool. The stream is prevented from flowing onward, and the dependent Life downstream begins to suffer. It loses its vibrancy, and begins to die. Of course, the stream cannot be stopped, for soon, the water must find new channels around this obstruction, and so, in time, it does. They say:

> Are you getting the picture? There is no ceasing of the flow. There is only the placing of obstructions—and there is, you will agree, some enjoyment in the activity of this—that temporarily stop the flow, and eventually change its course. Now, there is no problem here, as long as you allow that this is what is occurring. Enjoy the fun of your *what ifs* and release the seriousness you have attached to the game of it all. We trust we are making some sense here.

We wish now to address a question of timing. We have shown you the ultimate evolution of your glass house, and that is, as it will be with you, to return to the Earth from which it was created. The confusion is this—that you are the managers of the time frame in which this will occur. We will weave in another of our earlier points, and that is the creation of tension in yourselves, and in the home itself, surrounding what you call its upkeep. Allow this possibility—that you are, with your worry and concern and magnified vision, actually hastening that which you are working so hard to prevent. We recognize that given the harshness and variety of natural conditions that prevail in that most beautiful spot upon the planet, there is a wear and tear factor constantly working its alchemy on all that is exposed to it. Attend to what calls most loudly to you, but release your constant vigilance and the intensity of your focus on the many things that can go wrong. There is no wrong in this most natural of processes; it is simply that the processes must be kept at bay to preserve both your comfort and your investment. That is all. Recognize that were you to absent yourselves completely from the scene leaving all to its destiny, there would be no difficulty at all. Remove the observer/participant, and any thought of problem vanishes as well!

We do realize that we are making light of what in human terms is serious business, and we do so only to offer you a shift of perception. In effect, we ask that you ease the laser focus that you each carry within you that scouts, moment to moment, for anything that might need fixing. We are not suggesting you ignore, just hold more gently, order your priorities, and ask for help when needed. We recognize with great appreciation your love and honouring of this place and the magic of its energetic gifts; we honour you for the love and care and gratitude that pour constantly from you. In doing so, you have set up a cycle of reciprocity with this place that is ever intensifying and accelerating. You are so intimately woven into this exchange. It is moving indeed to witness.

At this point, they are showing me a picture that can best be described as a life cycle picture out of a biology text, as if painted by the artist Bev Doolittle. It's like a wheel of energy, and it moves through each of you, your land, trees, plants, flowers, deer, quail, birds, insects. As the energy flows, there are changes. Winds blow, rain falls, sun shines, plants lie flat, tree branches move and crack and some crash down. Deer are born and browse and come to your deck for treats and die…cycle is contained within the larger moving cycle. Then, I see an energetic flow between the two of you, within this. It circulates from each of your hearts to the other then back again. It's complicated, but you have this between you. At the same time, you are in the larger cycle, and you are also holding that larger cycle as well. From this, I understand that it is your presence, that in weaving yourselves into what exists there, you have actually enlivened everything. You have awakened your land, and brought it to life in a way that it was not alive before.

> And, you see that you yourselves have been awakened. That is the land's gift to you. Do you realize and recognize that the pace of your own discovery has accelerated greatly since you placed yourselves in harmonious co-habitation with the land? Think back, and you will know the truth of this.
>
> You wonder—Would it be wise to release our hold upon this land, its ownership, to free ourselves from the 'tyranny' of its demands? And we say to you, there will come a time when it will release its ownership of you! When it does so, you will feel it instantly. And at that time, there will be an ease felt in your decision to stay or to go, for then, it really will not matter. Until then, be easy. Watch for the traps of the Mind that tend to obscure the joy that is ever available to you. It takes only a moment of stillness to connect you to the Source of All That Is. It's true that this connection is available anywhere, but we must acknowledge that there are places where it is so much easier. You have found that place upon the Earth, one of many, but one that has called you to it. It is your home, for it has assisted each of you to find the home that dwells inside you.

I ask if there are any last words, any more to be said today. They show me a picture of your place with both of you working outside at separate tasks, but the energetic flow they describe above just is, with no effort, no doing. They are also showing disturbance, other people and machines and some noise on the periphery. Each of you looks up, then, you look at each other. There is a flash of annoyance, based in fear of change. Almost at the same instant, you shrug, the worry leaves, and you both smile knowingly at each other, as if you share the biggest and best kept secret. The energy between you intensifies. And you each turn back to your work.

At this point, I know the journey is complete. The scene fades, and I am back with my Power Animal. I thank him for this wonderful journey, and he tells me to remind you to read this with care, that there are many messages woven within it. I thank him again, and return to the room where I am working.

I thought it would be interesting to include Anne's thoughtful comments upon her receipt of the journey.

The journey has done the most valuable thing for us, and that is to connect us to Truth. I will try to explain.

I have for so long thought that we were working on this property, that its maintenance as a residence for ourselves and all of the wild life was somehow a result of our work here; however, through the Journey we are now able to see that this place on the Earth is actually ***our*** *opportunity. It is* ***our*** *place of healing, and when we look back at how it has changed us, as we were Guided to do, the amount of maintenance, renovation, and stewardship that the Land has worked on us is remarkable.*

As we were reminded, Nature, as it manifests here, demonstrates to us that "all is good" in the sense that it is "as it is." Winds blow, the sun smolders, deer are born and die, robins become dinner for hawks, and all happens with very little struggle. That is a current theme. To allow everything to be as it is, to respond appropriately, but to give up the struggle. When I first recognized that, I was concerned—"If one gives up vigilance, how does one avoid complacency?" I see now that there is a way to enter the flow, to respond, not react. I feel we are just beginning the training, and to that end, the land has not yet given up its hold on us. It feels as though we are at the beginning of our curriculum, and yet we know it could release us in a heartbeat. I am sure we will have no problem recognizing when we have been "given notice." The interesting thing is that the very issues that were driving us away, as our fear was stimulated, are the very issues that we now see as huge opportunities for all that is important in Life. After all, perhaps the aim of Life itself is not to be comfortable in material reality. Hmmmm, imagine that!

Isolation from Nature

Winter 2006

When we moved from a remote country property to an older suburb of Calgary, our young daughters had their first experience of an urban neighbourhood school. One day the elder returned, disgusted, from a field trip with her class to Fish Creek Provincial Park. "Can you believe it?" she remarked. "Those kids don't even know what moss is!"

Throughout my life, I have been both enlivened and soothed by connecting with nature. Because we see many who seem disconnected not only from the natural world, but from themselves as well, several of my colleagues and I chose the following journey topic. Here is the answer that was offered to me.

INTENTION

Many of us live isolated from nature.
What are the consequences of this?

I TRAVEL ALONG THE FOREST PATH IN THE LOWER WORLD. From our vantage point on the path, we view a baby lying naked on a rock. The rock is slightly indented, cradling the baby. The sun shines down on the child, warming its skin, but not so hot as to burn. The baby is completely part of nature in this environment. It plays happily in this innocent oneness. The trees, in full leaf, rustle lightly in the breeze, and seem protective of this little one. The baby is fed from a woman's breast, and it is indicated that this too, is completely natural, a part of the caring for and support of the baby. We walk on. Along the path I see the images that have appeared before and spoken their messages in a past journey, an owl, a snake with the jewel in its throat, a ladybug, a deer. We pass on to the clearing where White Cloud and Shining Moon are waiting. We greet each other, and I am surprised to see Shining Moon, as I have only encountered her in the World Below the Lower World. It seems that both will attend to the question, which I pose to them. They begin to speak:

> We have brought you to this clearing where you have been before, where you received your story of the North, a creation story, so to speak. We know that this clearing is completely aligned to your experience, or one of your many experiences of nature—it is pristine. A variety of tree species mingle here, both those that lose their leaves in a riot of colour every fall, and those that do not. When you peer closely at the bark of any one of these, you can see the industrious working of insects. Others fly through the air, we catch their hums, or songs, or sounds. Others labour under rocks, invisible to us unless we disturb their shelter. Birds of every description call from the treetops, build their nests, raise their young, and then fledge them, as is the order of progression through the cycle. Everywhere we look, with every sense to which we give our attention, we are aware of Life. The very sensitive may even hear the sound that grass makes as it pushes through earth and begins its growth towards the Sun. And we, as observers and also as participants in the cycle, we have learned to thrive here. Food is provided, although we must seek it and develop our knowing and expertise in obtaining it. Shelters can be constructed and de-constructed with ease, our children can be born, and are nurtured by all that exists around us. And yet, we are, of course, painting a rather idealized picture for you; recognize that because we are part of the never-ending cycle, because we are, as it were, cells in the great construct of the Universe, we are subject to the natural laws that, from the outside, bring death, disease, discomfort, and loss as well. Know that.
>
> Now, to your question. Let us look first at the assumption—Many live isolated from nature. We can agree readily, when we consider that this pristine environment in which you now stand no longer exists in such a form upon your planet. In attempting

to manage all for the perceived benefit of a few, much has been lost. The availability of such spaces even remotely offering what is provided here has been drastically reduced, and is in great peril of complete destruction. We observe that in the duality that is so common in your species, there are those who fight to protect such spaces, even as the powers to destroy them increase with intensified velocity. Those protectors hold in their hearts two things—a sense of grief and great foreboding of what will result when all such wild places have been removed, and a further sense that, if they can just hold on to some of these places, through their consciousness and example, others will be ignited, and, in effect, the tide can be reversed. We see the pain and caring that these beings embody, we feel their love, their angst, their desperation, and yes, their hope, but we say to them—reversal has never been the way of evolution. There is no going back, there is no return to the imagined paradise of previous times, there is, in fact, nothing wrong. The orbs of existence continue their tumbling movements through the void, each an encapsulated world and also an object woven into the web of the expanding universe. Separate and one, a divine paradox of existence.

When you ask of the consequences, we imagine that you are requesting specifically information of the effect on those sentient beings on your planet, and in particular, mankind. Such a question is huge in its scope. First, we will remind you that you are very aware of the most obvious of consequences. When, through natural change and the accelerated change perpetrated by those who alter the chemistry of the air that you breathe, the water that you drink, and the food that you eat, you can see how quickly aberrations in structure of sentient beings occur, how readily disease forms take hold of healthy tissues, how whole species vanish from those regions where before they were plentiful. This does not need explanation at this time. Alter the environment, and all that depends on a beneficial inter-

Green Man

Green Man
(watercolour, 1994)

'Green Man' is really a portrait of my beautiful son, Logan, at about eight years of age, dressed in a halo of greenery. Logan has grown up to be a fervent environmentalist. He practices sustainable living, striving to leave only the faintest footprints of his passing, encouraging others to do the same. It is possible, he tells us, to give back more than we take, thus leaving the earth richer than it was before our arrival. Imagine that!

relationship with that environment will begin to alter too. The physical system of many cannot adjust quickly enough to thrive in what has been newly created, for the changes in the environment speed ahead of the consequent changes in structure and function of those who live there. This is not to say that all is lost. Many will abandon their recognizable physical forms, it's true. But it does not necessarily follow that their very *existence* is threatened. Change and alteration can happen instantaneously in dis-embodied beings, so for many, relinquishing the body is the preferred and expedient way. (*We feel your internal struggle with this notion, for you yourself are one who grieves the loss and passing of both environments and beings.*) We are attempting to provide you with the clear sense that what has passed will, in time, when environments are suitable, re-create themselves, with the assistance of the unifying force, in entirely new ways. Allow the possibility of this within your mind, and you will feel soothed.

And now, to the consequences for the human species upon your planet at this time. We remind you that, what is true for others, as we spoke of previously, is true for you as well. You were created from the Mother as part of the Mother; because she has been such a good Mother, she has become, in effect, the agent of her own destruction. She is being devoured by her own children. (*There is so much coming here. The sense I have is that this is related to the mushrooming population. Everyone—no matter what their means, country, education, etc.—all are participating in this process of devouring that which birthed and sustained us for so long. No one group is specifically to blame; we are more alike in this than we think!*)

I ask if there can be any information given specifically about the ultimate consequences to living isolated from nature. They are saying:

> Can you see that your question is flawed? No one lives isolated from nature, for the word isolation suggests a lack of interaction. What we are demonstrating here is that there is no isolation. It is not possible. Every aspect is in constant communion with every other aspect. Nothing is untouched or unaffected, nothing. All truly is One; isolation is impossible.

I ask, then, if they can offer a picture of the future for humankind upon the planet. White Cloud and Shining Moon look at each other and smile that knowing look that parents share when their naive children ask a question to which the answer is so blatantly obvious. They give a visual picture. Our beautiful planet, seen from space, with its clear colours, blues, and greens, blacks, browns, then bands of cloud, then haze and smoke from fires burning. Fast forward to the planet almost completely obscured, the outline visible though. Like a dog that has come out of a lake, it gives a shudder and then a series of shakes. Sprays and sprays of droplets fly off into space, some settle back on the body of the Earth. Fast forward to the haze or mists clearing, Earth re-revealed, but the configuration of colours has changed. I am reminded of the colours I saw in the desert of Australia, the many shades of pink, orange and red, but patches of blue and green as well.

I sense the information is complete for now. I thank the two teachers, and embrace them. There is no sense that they are disturbed by the information they have provided. In fact, they are remarkably serene.

I travel with Diamondback along the path, past the baby, and then we say good-bye. I thank him for being the guide on this journey.

The Nature of the Universe in which I Live

The words of this journey lift me up whenever I feel helpless and overwhelmed by the frantic, depressing, and often contradictory messages that are regularly offered up as true comment on the state of our beautiful planet.

May you be inspired to explore the nature of the universe in which you live, and may you be uplifted by the vision shared in mine.

INTENTION

Please describe the nature of the universe in which I live.

THE NATURE OF YOUR UNIVERSE is filled with unending possibility. This of course is shaped, as is each individual universe, by your own perception. It cannot be otherwise. You have, throughout your life, received conditioning that tells you this is good, this is bad, this exists, this does not. The conditioning settles deeply in the cells, in the energy emanations, and shapes that perception. For many, there is no escape, but you have been fortunate. Your orientation towards joy, your willingness to question, the appearance of teachers of all kinds at critical points in your life—all have conspired to assist in the expansion of that universe beyond the narrow scope of the conditioned thoughts and fears. You have discovered that with each layer that is pulled away, your universe expands; its clarity reveals more and more its crystalline essence.

The universe is rich with possibility and of course we are not referring strictly to opportunity and advancement in the material way. This universe is, in every direction, teeming with information that may come directly, or through the myriad of teachers who are available to access. No one lifetime is sufficient to absorb and integrate the range of this availability. The boundaries of this universe have lost their fixedness; they shimmer and expand with each new revelation. Any limitations—and there are some—come from the system's challenge to keep pace with what can be provided. This is not lack, but simply part of the process of expansion. Within the orb of this universe, it is important to maintain the everyday rituals of the simplicity of life such as driving a car, walking, sharing with community—all that is necessary to care for yourself and your responsibilities in the physical world. Each supports and does not interfere with the other. This is the balance of Heaven and Earth.

We remind you to approach each new day with ever widening open eyes.

Study the Ancient Ways...

Marilyn Geddes & Cynthia Mackenzie

About the Author

MARILYN GEDDES has lived and worked in and around Calgary, Alberta for most of her life. Her love for animals was inspired by her father, who, during her early years, read to her nightly from his favourite book, *The Fireside Book of Dog Stories.* Later, he supported her, in spite of her mother's stringent objections, when she brought home numerous animal friends, including five small, multicoloured chicks that had been dyed 'in the egg' in honour of Easter. The patience of all was tested when they quickly grew into raucous roosters, with full run of the family basement!

Marilyn currently resides in a 'woodland in the city' home in Calgary with her husband. When possible, they spend time with their wonderful and beloved children who have grown up and embarked on their own adventures. Marilyn's joy is to be outdoors with human and animal friends, appreciating with great gratitude the beauty that suffuses all of creation. Her favourite pastime is riding her horse, Patchy, over the rolling shortgrass prairie near the Porcupine Hills, southwest of the city. Her younger daughter often accompanies her on her horse, Joker. Her older daughter joins them whenever she visits Alberta.

Marilyn has been a shamanic practitioner for several years.

About the Illustrator

CYNTHIA MACKENZIE lives happily in the ever-expanding city of Calgary, which she claims is the best place in the world.

Cynthia feels very fortunate to have chosen painting as a profession. Not one for formal structure, she lives each day as she chooses. She delights in saying 'yes' to any adventure offered at a moment's notice. Whether making art or working at her part-time life coaching practice, she is immersed in a creative process that offers her balance and satisfaction.

Cynthia loves to bring friends together for evenings of conversation, good food and much wine. Though her two children have launched themselves into different but equally interesting directions, they remain closely connected to her.

Travelling where she chooses, thinking and sharing without fear whatever comes, and living her life as she wishes, leave Cynthia thankful every day for the freedom to do so. A day may begin and end with chocolate cake.

MARILYN AND CYNTHIA MET AT A WORKSHOP where many had gathered to sit with Paul Lowe, a spiritual teacher. During one session, Paul directed his attention to Cynthia, who was seated in the front row. He indicated that she had much in common with the woman sitting behind her, and suggested they meet. Later, Cynthia introduced herself to Marilyn, or perhaps it was the other way around. Now close and trusted friends, they have been fellow seekers, travelling companions, confidantes, business partners, and most recently, creative collaborators. The two share their love of family and friends, animal companions, the natural world, good conversation, and movies. Cynthia frequently joins Marilyn in riding across the prairie.

Selected Reading

Boone, J.A. (1977). *Letters to strongheart.* Harrington Park, NJ: Robert H. Sommer.

———. (1954). *Kinship with all life.* New York, NY: Harper.

Daniels, J.Y. (2007). *Heeding the call: A personal journey to the sacred.* Calgary, AB: Hearthlight Publishing.

Hansard, C. (2002). *The Tibetan art of living: Wise body, mind, life.* New York, NY: Atria Books/Simon & Schuster, Inc.

Perkins, J. (1997). *Shapeshifting: Techniques for global and personal transformation.* Rochester, VT: Inner Traditions/Destiny Books.

———. (1994). *The world is as you dream it: Teachings from the Amazon and Andes.* Rochester, VT: Inner Traditions/Destiny Books.

To purchase additional copies of *Ask the Very Beasts*,
please visit us online at:

www.rattlesnakebooks.com

To view artworks by Cynthia Mackenzie,
please visit her studio online at:

www.cynthiamackenzie.com

Correspondence may be sent to:

Rattlesnake Books
c/o 871 Cannell Road SW
Calgary, Alberta, Canada T2W 1T5